Ink Trails II

De Tour
John Tobin Nevill

Mackinaw City
Frances Margaret Fox

Walloon Lake
Ernest Miller Hemingway

Suttons Bay
James Beardsley Hendryx

Traverse City
Harold Titus

Manton
Julia Ann Moore

Mecosta
Russell Amos Kirk

Grand Rapids
Constance Maybury Rourke

East Lansing
Ray Stannard Baker
Glendon Swarthout
Emma Shore Thornton

Port Huron
Mary Frances Doner

Holland
Arnold Mulder

Detroit
Donald Joseph Goines
Edgar Albert Guest
Orlando Bolivar Willcox

Jackson
Della Thompson Lutes

Adrian
Allan John Braithwaite Seager

Ink Trails II

Michigan's Famous and Forgotten Authors

DAVE DEMPSEY *and* JACK DEMPSEY

Michigan State University Press

East Lansing

∞ The paper used in this publication meets the minimum requirements
of ANSI/NISO Z39.48-1992 (R 1997) (Permanence of Paper).
Michigan State University Press
East Lansing, Michigan 48823-5245

Printed and bound in the United States of America.

22 21 20 19 18 17 16   1 2 3 4 5 6 7 8 9 10

Library of Congress Cataloging-in-Publication is available
ISBN: 978-1-61186-207-2 (pbk.)
ISBN: 978-1-60917-493-4 (ebook: PDF)
ISBN: 978-1-62895-266-7 (ebook: ePub)
ISBN: 978-1-62896-266-6 (ebook: Kindle)

Frontispiece map by E. White
Book and cover design by Erin Kirk New
Original cover art by Erin Kirk New includes a map by Ellen White and
work from ©iStockphoto.com / Cheryl Graham.

G green press Michigan State University Press is a member of the Green Press
Initiative and is committed to developing and encouraging ecologi-
cally responsible publishing practices. For more information about the
Green Press Initiative and the use of recycled paper in book publishing,
please visit www.greenpressinitiative.org.

Visit Michigan State University Press at www.msupress.org

To gentle souls Barbara Ann Cameron and
Michael Cameron, until we meet again

Contents

Preface

Dave Dempsey

You could spend a lifetime exploring Michigan and never come close to discovering the entire wealth of beauty in the 36 million acres of land that make up the state. And you could spend a lifetime exploring the work of authors associated with Michigan and never consume their riches, often buried like treasure.

In this second visit to the dens of storytellers linked with Michigan, my brother and I have learned that the well of Wolverine State literary talent is seemingly inexhaustible. We have tried not to slight the giants like Hemingway while unearthing the works of forgotten women and men who, in their day, made a contribution to letters.

These relative unknowns fascinate me. Some harvested vast sums from their writing, some very little. Some created for four or five decades, while some had a single burst of writing and went silent. What all had in common was a keen personal insight they wanted to share with an audience that loved words and stories as much as each of them did. It should not have surprised me as much as it did that these insights were almost always universal, and are almost always meaningful today. These authors and their works matter.

I learned something else. As someone who loves the natural beauty of Michigan, I have been struck by how many of the authors I encountered were moved by the character of the state's outdoors. Allan Seager celebrated the special light of his homeland in Lenawee County. Frances Margaret Fox was captivated by the majesty of the Straits of Mackinac. Harold Titus was passionate about reforesting the state. The wonder of the dunes of the Lower Peninsula's west coast transfixed Arnold Mulder. In some way, whether they were conscious of it or not, Michigan was an uncredited coauthor of many of their works.

Michigan is many things, and among them it is a cradle of literary talent. I hope this second volume of *Ink Trails* not only inspires readers to track down some of the profiled authors and their past works, but also inspires authors with Michigan connections struggling to bring forth new works. We will be poorer if they do not persevere in turning their singular stories into words.

Preface

Jack Dempsey

When *Ink Trails* was first conceived in 2008 and then made its appearance in late summer 2012, hardly anyone was talking about Michigan being the "Trail State." That identity isn't new, only revived: these peninsulas have drawn people into unparalleled experiences ever since the earliest pathways were blazed by Native Americans on land and lake. Our literary heritage has proven to be as robust and diverse and as geographically dispersed as the natural splendor found everywhere.

This sequel contains more rediscoveries of authors for whom Michigan served as inspiration. As in the first volume, some are well-known but their full story is not. Others are obscure. The work of at least one, Willcox, faded and was hidden for over a century. Following all of their paths has been illuminating and a real privilege, especially alongside a brother whose own ink trails derive so much from this place.

Each of their stories shows one thing or another essential about this Great Lakes State. Here are abiding treasures, both in triumph and in dolor, that cannot be alienated from the heart or hidden from the pen.

Acknowledgments

Family, friends, and acquaintances offered up suggestions for inclusion if there was to be an *Ink Trails II*. To all of you, our thanks for being caught up in this journey as well. And for those disappointed by the absence of Hemingway in the first, we hope to have doubled your pleasure here.

Appreciation is owed to many fine people at museums, historical societies, and repositories of books and periodicals throughout Michigan. Special thanks go to these: Bentley Historical Library, Clarke Historical Library at Central Michigan University, Grand Rapids Public Library, Jackson District Library, Library of Michigan, Michigan eLibrary, and Plymouth District Library.

Several sources on Michigan authors have come to light since we first began this project. All are helpful; none is comprehensive. An article in *Michigan History* magazine evaluated Moore; a presentation at the Historical Society of Michigan Conference in fall 2014 talked of Kirk. *The Dictionary of Midwestern Literature* published by Indiana University Press, though compendious, still lacks entries on authors we discovered.

Our thanks to DeeAnn Greene-Marszulak and Mary Obuchowski for invaluable guidance and assistance.

To Jacqueline Tinney, our gratitude for dedication to research, manuscript preparation, and friendship. To Jason Masteller, thanks for invaluable assistance with images, technology, and encouragement.

Dave thanks Jennifer Morris for her support and integrity, and Joe Vander-Meulen, Derwin Rushing, and Tom Vance for a lifetime of friendship.

Jack thanks Suzzanne Dempsey and Anna Kathryn Door for their unfailing love and support.

Both Dave and Jack express their appreciation and love to their brother Tom.

Last, thank you to the wonderful people at Michigan State University Press who have brought these volumes into print.

Ink Trails II

Baker and Thornton

Liberal Artists

Ray Stannard Baker: April 17, 1870–July 12, 1946
Born in Lansing; graduate of the Agricultural College; studied at University of Michigan; lived in East Lansing

Emma Shore Thornton: July 10, 1908–March 24, 1998
Taught at Michigan State University; lived in East Lansing

The farming heritage of the institution originally known as the Agricultural College of the State of Michigan might suggest that it is the seat of conservative thought in the Great Lakes State. Far from the industrial cauldrons of southeast Michigan, straddling the low banks of the placid Red Cedar, the school would seem to naturally breed believers in traditional ways. Ray Stannard Baker could have been such a disciple. He was born just a few years after the Civil War into a primarily rural America, one of six sons in a close-knit but far from wealthy Lansing family. By the age of nineteen, he had graduated from the school in East Lansing and headed on to Ann Arbor to study law at the great university on the Huron River. As a diversion, Baker attended a "Rapid Writing" course for hopefuls in newspaper reporting, and it suggested how he might earn money enough to complete his legal studies. He spent the summer of 1892 in Chicago reporting on the Columbian Exposition. Instead of serving only as a short-term post, the

Ray Stannard Baker was an 1889 graduate of the Agricultural College of the State of Michigan, muckraker, winner of the Pulitzer Prize for his biography of Woodrow Wilson, and author of paeans to rural living under the pseudonym David Grayson.

work enchanted him, and he stayed on after the fair as a reporter to write about the city and its people.

Baker's enthusiasm arose not from the greatness of his urban surroundings; rather, the winter of 1893–94 brought an economic crisis, and he found subject matter in soup kitchens, tenements, and public assemblies, decrying widespread poverty. The contrast between the glitz of the Exposition and the plight of the impoverished provided daily fodder for his reporting for the *News Record*. He went to Ohio to report on a proposed poor people's march on Washington, D.C. Upon his return, writing about the Pullman strike of 1894, perhaps the first truly national labor-management conflict, brought Baker's name into prominence. When the next assignment was the criminal beat, he decided to work on a novel instead, hoping it would sell enough to enable him and his new bride to set up a happy home.

Chicago was the birthplace of Jessie Irene Beal, a classmate in East Lansing he had known since she was fifteen. She had earned her BS in agriculture in 1890 (the only woman in a class of twenty-two) and also attended the University of Michigan from 1892 to 1894. She was the daughter and only surviving child of Professor William James Beal, Adrian native and graduate of the university. He had studied under the famous Asa Gray at Harvard University and was teaching at the University of Chicago when his daughter

Emma Gertrude Shore Thornton, a daughter of the Midwest, was a poet, professor at Michigan State University, and emissary for peace and goodwill. Courtesy of Janet S. Boysen.

was born. The following year, the family relocated to Michigan when he was hired as professor of botany at the State Agricultural College. Beal founded the botanical garden that bears his name, and in 1889 he became director of the Michigan Forestry Commission. The professor's wife, Hannah, "was connected with the affairs of the [college] for nearly forty years, when it was new and struggling with only six professors . . . Cut off by three miles of rough road, the College was forced to live much to itself. Its life was that of a large family and of that family many of the students remember Mrs. Beal, truly, as the mother."[1]

Ray and Jessie were married on January 2, 1896, in Michigan, and soon began their wedded life back in the Windy City. After his would-be Great American Novel was rejected by Harper's, Baker spent hours tearing it "chapter by chapter into the smallest possible fragments" and "pushing them into my growing wastebasket with my fist." But he did not despair; an assignment to write a column called "Shop Talks on the Wonders of the Crafts" might provide fresh insight into the new industrial world and help make a reimagined novel publishable. One day he arrived at the office to find quite a surprise on his desk: a paperback compilation of the Shop Talk columns. Without really trying, he had written a book after all, even though it did not credit him as author.

This unanticipated success spurred him to fashion a short story for credited publication, which appeared in *Youth's Companion*. Soon Baker was writing and publishing more, devoting a week of the couple's customary summer vacation in Michigan to write a five-part tale of the north woods—and receive a fat check for $250. He wrote for *McClure's* magazine an account of his Uncle Lafayette's role in the Lincoln assassination proceedings, and the publisher invited him to New York City. The trip resulted in a position as editor and contributor—necessitating a move to New York.

Baker ran in exciting new circles, meeting notables with names such as Roosevelt. Although he never felt a calling to join the military, he found it easy to write about Teddy's exploits in Cuba and the stories of other contemporary martial heroes. Perhaps his family lineage—his father, who was a Civil War veteran; a grandfather who served in the War of 1812; a great-grandfather who served under Anthony Wayne; and a great-great-grandfather, Captain Remember Baker, who was a Revolutionary War peer of Ethan Allen—gave him inspiration. Within two decades, war became a central aspect of his life and career.

Despite the job in New York, and regardless of what seemed a solid reputation, failure to produce a *Moby-Dick* or *Adventures of Huckleberry Finn* enervated him. He began to suffer from depression. The Bakers tried living in Arizona, and then he sought the sun alone in California, but the cure did not take. He returned to New York and to subjects that failed to enthuse. In 1902, everything began to change.

While Baker was traveling in search of healing, his wife and children moved to her parents' home near the college in East Lansing. Nearby, "a small settlement had been started on an old Michigan farm. It was not even, as yet, a village." Here, Baker acquired "a small white house with room for a garden behind it, and we moved in." He had loved the "open farming and forest country all about" as a student, and now he discovered it could serve as "a quiet spot where I could work." These efforts were not focused on social criticism or formulaic magazine pieces or serials; it was work on what he most wanted to do. Here, he planned out a new life. He fitted up one corner of a bedroom as a study and began to write something altogether different from his efforts in previous genres.

Like the canoeists in this late nineteenth-century scene on the Red Cedar, Baker enjoyed the waterway as a student and later while on family excursions. Photo A001736, courtesy of Michigan State University Archives and Historical Collections.

Part of the emotional crisis had arisen from a falling-out with the president. Baker's continuing exposés of workingmen's conditions and attacks on railroad interests were designed to aid Teddy in curtailing the abuses of management. Roosevelt ripped this reporting as overly negative and damaging to the national interest. Referring to Baker's kind of writing as "muckraking," Roosevelt sensed that times had changed, that Americans were fatigued of the story line, and that political points were to be gained by repudiating such journalism. Disillusioned, Baker retreated to Michigan.

"I went home utterly beaten down with weariness, worn out physically and mentally," he recounted. But he had a home in the countryside, near the college and his mentors, not far from his father and Dr. Beal. Baker found the nearby marshes exquisite; walks through woods proved refreshing. His home life had become more satisfactory than ever, much more than anything he had known in the big city. He enjoyed abundant time playing with his four children, reliving the youthful experiences afforded by his father, imitating that example. The family had regular Sunday picnics, routinely swam in Pine Lake (now Lake Lansing), and boated frequently on the Red Cedar.

The community embraced its celebrity reporter. He helped found the "Peoples Church," where in October 1909, a cornerstone was laid in the "College Grove" development carved out of the old Parmalee farm, three doors east of the intersection at Abbot Road and Grand River Avenue.

As he became reinvigorated, Baker became one of the owners of *The American Magazine* with fellow investigative journalists Lincoln Steffens and Ida M. Tarbell. Unusual for its era, the periodical took on racial issues. In 1908 Baker authored five articles on contemporary African American life, exposing the effects of Jim Crow laws, confronting the horror of lynching, and once again revealing the hopelessness of poverty. The pieces became a book, *Following the Color Line*. There, he wrote:

> If the white man sets an example of non-obedience to law, of non-enforcement of law, and of unequal justice, what can be expected of the Negro? A criminal father is a poor preacher of homilies to a wayward son. The Negro sees a man, white or black, commit murder and go free, over and over again in all these lynching counties. Why should he fear to murder?

All the while he was living in East Lansing and commuting to New York to the magazine offices at 141–147 Fifth Avenue.

And, all the while, he was continuing on the novel—two, in fact. One day, invited to forward good new material, he discovered enjoyment in writing a different kind of story. It did not muckrake or expose the dark underbelly of America, and it was not forced, as were his previous attempts at fiction. This kind of story came naturally, for it was about nature, and everything he "knew about country life poured into my mind." He enumerated the sources of inspiration, including:

> My winters teaching school in farming communities in Michigan, bits and strays from my years in an agricultural college, and most vivid of all, the experiences of recent years in our own home in the village of East Lansing. I found myself writing about the interest and beauty of the natural scene—fields and hills, rivers and forests, everything in nature that stirs a man's soul.

Three weeks later he had substantial chapters in hand. Not fully confident of their worth, he sent them off under a pseudonym, David Grayson. Soon came a telegram advising him, "Manuscript a delight. Bully boy. Send more chapters."

As David Grayson, Baker would write nine volumes to popular acclaim, selling millions of copies. During the early years of the twentieth century, an epoch ushered in with urbanization and the first worldwide war, the virtues of the simple rural life and the essential goodness of humanity in nature played well to readers. Grayson was no reactionary; he had an open mind to progress, asserting that "the only sure conclusion we can reach is this: life changes." One review stated:

> Grayson's followers will find further reminiscences, observations, commentary in this new collection of articles on country living. There are bees, onions, trees, birds, fish, part-time farming, books, quotations, there are the joys of manual labor, the delights of country living, the leisurely learning, the philosophy of growing older not unhappily, the constant rejuvenation from the earth, the lessons of illness and the importance of inner peace to face the world of today. Contemplative, soothing this.[2]

Paralleling his Grayson work and while writing for *American Magazine*, Baker made the acquaintance of President Woodrow Wilson. The two largely shared the same foreign policy views and hit it off. Recognizing Baker's communication abilities, the president appointed him special commissioner for the State Department, enabling his attendance at postwar conferences on the League of Nations where he effectively served as the president's European press secretary. Their close relationship led to Baker being asked to edit Wilson's papers and write his biography, a task he readily accepted. In 1940, Baker won the Pulitzer Prize in Biography for the multiyear, multivolume *Woodrow Wilson: Life and Letters*. It was quite a year: other winners included John Steinbeck in the Novel category for *Grapes of Wrath* and Carl Sandburg in History for *Lincoln: The War Years*. Four years later, Baker worked as a technical adviser on the Twentieth Century Fox film *Wilson*. The movie garnered several Oscars.

Baker won no awards for his work as David Grayson, only a form of immortality. One still can find Grayson quotes on the Internet. They have an essential homeliness: "What we get in the city is not life, but what someone else tells us about life." "Back of tranquility lies always conquered unhappiness." "We are bored not by living, but by not living enough." "I do not have to make over the universe; I have only to do my job, great or small, and to look often at the trees and the hills and the sky, and be friendly with all men." By the time he died in 1946, after years of illness, Baker's journey from the muddy paths of East Lansing to the centers of power in New York and Washington could truly be considered amazing.

Ray Stannard Baker continued to amass accolades after death. He is enshrined in the Michigan Journalism Hall of Fame for his groundbreaking work as a reporter. In 1946, his alma mater saluted its graduate with a grand distinguished alumni award, later naming a building for him. It had not failed to recognize him while alive: in 1917, he received an honorary doctorate of laws. Though he lived his last years in Amherst, Massachusetts, Baker continued to treasure the mid-Michigan community that had nurtured his soul at a time when this was critical to his life and work.

In 1939 Baker showed his gratitude in paying the campus a final visit during the celebration of the fiftieth anniversary of his class's graduation. He called it "a rare experience"—high praise for someone who had conferred with presidents and won writing awards. His college experience did inspire him to write, and his words expressed fondness for the rural school instructors he'd learned so much from: "I can give it as my ripe opinion that few institutions of like size ever had a larger proportion of first-class teachers. I shall never cease to be thankful that it was my fortune to sit under them."[3] Whether writing as Baker or Grayson, his voice drew its timbre from a home in Michigan.

Emma Gertrude Shore was born near Rushmore, a tiny town in the far southwest corner of the rural plains of Minnesota, in the first decade of the twentieth century. When she was ten years old, her family moved to nearby Worthington, an only slightly more populous farming community. After public school she received a BA from Morningside College in Sioux City, Iowa; her circle of existence to this point encompassed about a hundred miles of flat earth marked by roads largely heading at right angles to each other.

Graduating in 1930 into the depth of the Depression, she moved to tiny Parker, South Dakota, teaching English and history and working in historical documentation for the Works Progress Administration. Six years later she married George Thornton while he was obtaining his doctorate at the

University of Nebraska; they had met in high school. The couple moved to West Lafayette, Indiana, in 1939 when George obtained a professorship at Purdue. They relocated again in 1944 to Ann Arbor when he decided to attend law school. Emma taught at a one-room schoolhouse on Geddes Road east of town, near present-day US-23. A family story relates that one of her students was the son of Harry Bennett, the legendary Ford Motor Company official. The "legend" rings true since the Bennett "castle" is only a half mile away, off Geddes.

In 1946 the Thorntons put down roots in East Lansing so that George could start his practice. After so many previous stops, it became their home for the next half century. They first attended the Peoples Church, then in 1949 helped found the Unitarian Congregation of Greater Lansing, hosting it in their home in 1950. Beginning in 1961, Emma took a position instructing students in the Michigan State University American Thought and Language program (ATL). Fifteen years later, despite the lack of a graduate degree, she retired as assistant professor emerita. The dozen-year delay in resuming a role as educator came from her devotion to raising two "chosen" children, a boy adopted at eight months and a girl when three, on a full-time basis.

While at Purdue, Emma had first participated in a writing group that inspired her to try poetry. Her efforts focused on the environs and the populace she had always known, the Midwest and its "grassroots people."[4] Her first collection of poems was published by the ATL department in 1975 with the dedication "For Jerry Thornton in recognition of her effort in the classroom and in poetry."[5]

ATL sought to teach critical reading, writing, and cultural analysis skills to undergraduates at Michigan State. Thornton thrived in the department. She endeared herself to colleagues and students, and one of her closest associates was Pauline Gordon Adams, spouse of World War II veteran and Distinguished Professor Walter Adams. He served as MSU's thirteenth president; Pauline served as the university's first lady during his term. The two female professors collaborated on several works focused on "the workings of the democratic process through the lives of ordinary people." One study was of populist Sarah E. Van De Vort Emery, a slim volume of just over one hundred pages. They also jointly conducted *An Inquiry into the Process of Collaboration*, prompted by curiosity about their ability to write together:

This study, a tentative and preliminary exploration of how two or more people write together, began as a very small dinghy cast upon what turns out to be a very wide sea. Soon after articles we had written together appeared and were read or heard, we noticed something quite surprising. Raised eyebrows. Quasi-queries. Explicit questions. "How do you work together?" "Who does what?" "How do you ever get cohesion?" "How do you reconcile differences?" At first, these reactions took us aback. Had the article's substance been so flimsy as to have been completely blown before the wind? Then it hit us. We had thought only of the product: the audience had been intrigued by the collaborative process.

Perhaps a world in constant conflict requires the example of two Midwesterners to teach it how to work collaboratively.

Professor Thornton's nonfiction work included a "bio-history" of the first state librarian for Michigan, Loleta Fyan. She authored a history of the Universalist Church in the community. *Ideas Have Consequences: 125 Years of the Liberal Tradition in the Lansing Area* recounted how the work of women of the church held the congregation together through difficult times. The couple became members of the combined Unitarian Universalist Church of Greater Lansing. They also aided the Liberal Religious Youth organization after its founding in 1954.

The last years of her life were difficult. She suffered from arthritis, cancer, and likely ALS and died after a long battle in 1998. George lived to be ninety-nine. Their ashes were given back to the earth at the Unitarian Universalist Church Memorial Garden in East Lansing.

The Thorntons left behind a legacy of peace and goodwill. They were benevolent people, characteristically hosting students left behind at school, one of whom was blind, during the Thanksgiving break. Their church maintains the George & Jerry Thornton Endowment Fund for Peace. Michigan State continues to offer the Emma Shore Thornton annual scholarship for high-achieving undergraduate and graduate American Indian students. She sketched and painted, but her true legacy remains small collections of poetry still in print.

Those poems were never meant for a large audience. In an oversized journal she mounted a compendium of typewritten poems—many, but not all, published—and passed it to her son and daughter-in-law with the humble suggestion that they were not "really very good by objective standards."

Despite that harsh judgment, she embraced their creation, for "I had joy in my own doing of it! And if you like sharing it, that multiplies the value immeasurably for me." Against the odds and her own evaluation, a 1983 anthology of Michigan literature included one of her pieces—the volume seeking to preserve work that tends "to fall between the cracks." Along with Hemingway, Lardner, and Roethke appears the writing of Emma Shore Thornton.

Her verse celebrates the unspoiled imagery of the Midwest. She wrote of the "sky-whipped blanket" of snow "on the roof opposite" in "This Time, Upgoing." The phrasing is simple and elegant, as in "a bright February morning with the blue-high sky present and accounted for," how "the frost rim grows on our fruitful days." Fall brought a different sort of emotion:

> I took a walk with October
> Under the broad, blue sky;
> And the golden love of October
> Is a mother to lay me by.

The onset of spring helped ease unavoidable grief into a renewed desire for survival: "What sings in the heart / Sends a glow to the brain." Michigan bird life helped inspire that song, as one poem relies on sparrows and finches, cardinals and chickadees, juncos and jays to fill the scenery. A poem entitled "Michigan Caprice" roots itself both in her birthplace and her Michigan home:

> The north wind wooshes from the west,
> And in the confusion great puffs of snow
> Like soft and fluffy whips of cream
> Abandon their harbors on tree limbs
> And sail off—perhaps to the ground.
> A clutter of crows whirl and scold
> and grandstand around,
> Filling the air with a raucous sound.
> Above all that a Minnesota blue reaches all
> the way to the sun.

Not all of her poems were naturalistic. One in *The Stone in My Pocket* ("A Single Telling Moment") celebrated the 1979 MSU basketball team, finding in their championship-caliber performance both a ballet of grace and a Niagara of power. Others in the volume are not so light-hearted. In a poem about her daughter entitled "Herself," Thornton wrote about how the girl "came into the house a waif / Her eyes, anxious pains" in contrast with "the waiting and open parental hopes." Gradually, though, the three-year-old begins to accept as she is accepted, though the process of it is a question pondered: "Was the answer in making the oatmeal, / tying the shoestrings, / sewing on buttons . . . ?" The title piece begins: "Where once I would have chosen one smooth and polished / I guess I now prefer a rock / that is rough, grainy, intractable and uneven /—like life."

Thornton's writing, like Baker's more prolific works, springing from the sturdy soil of the Midwest, raised up an earnest and useful crop, and died away to be unearthed by the curious. Both crossed from what passes as fact into fancy: Baker via Grayson, Thornton through poetry. Both empathized with others; both embraced liberality of thought. Both found near the Red Cedar in the heart of Michigan a place where their expressions flourished.

Of the two, Professor Thornton labored in much greater obscurity, though Baker's library has gathered much dust. Still, their epitaph is a common one, found in one of her poems, "All of Forever":

When Death comes and whispers to me,
"Your days are over,"
Let me say to him,
"I have lived in love,
        not in mere time.
I have fellowships afar,
        though you may say I have been nowhere."
He will ask, "Will your songs remain?"
I shall say, "I don't know;
I think not; I don't really care.
But this I know:
That often when I sang,
Often when I grieved,
Often when I loved—There was all I need of forever."

Works

RAY STANNARD BAKER

Shop Talks on the Wonders of the Crafts (Chicago: Chicago Record, 1895).

The Boy's Book of Inventions: Stories of the Wonders of Modern Science (New York: Doubleday, McClure, 1899).

Our New Prosperity (New York: Doubleday, McClure, 1900).

Seen in Germany (New York: McClure, Phillips, 1901).

Boys' Second Book of Inventions (New York: McClure, Phillips, 1903).

Adventures in Contentment (New York: Doubleday, Page, 1907) (as David Grayson).

Following the Color Line: An Account of Negro Citizenship in the American Democracy (New York: Doubleday, Page, 1908).

New Ideals in Healing (New York: Frederick A. Stokes, 1909).

The Spiritual Unrest (New York: Frederick A. Stokes, 1910).

Adventures in Friendship (New York: Doubleday, Page, 1910) (as David Grayson).

The Friendly Road: New Adventures in Contentment (New York: Doubleday, Page, 1913) (as David Grayson).

Hempfield: An American Novel (New York: Doubleday, Page, 1915) (as David Grayson).

Great Possessions: A New Series of Adventures (New York: Doubleday, Page, 1917) (as David Grayson).

What Wilson Did at Paris (Garden City: Doubleday, Page, 1919).

Woodrow Wilson and World Settlement, 3 vols. (Garden City: Doubleday, Page, 1922).

An American Pioneer in Science: The Life and Service of William James Beal (with Jessie B. Baker) (Amherst, MA: Privately printed, 1925).

Adventures in Understanding (New York: Doubleday, Page, 1925) (as David Grayson).

The Public Papers of Woodrow Wilson, 6 vols. (ed. with William E. Dodd) (New York: Harper & Bros., 1925–27).

Woodrow Wilson: Life and Letters, 8 vols. (Garden City, NY: Doubleday, Page; and Doubleday, Doran, 1927–39).

Adventures in Solitude (New York: Doubleday, Doran, 1931) (as David Grayson).

The Countryman's Year (New York: Doubleday, Doran, 1936) (as David Grayson).

Native American: The Book of My Youth (New York: Charles Scribner's Sons, 1941).

Under My Elm: Country Discoveries and Reflections (New York: Doubleday, Doran, 1942) (as David Grayson).

American Chronicle: The Autobiography of Ray Stannard Baker (New York: Charles
  Scribner's Sons, 1945).

EMMA SHORE THORNTON

"Heirs and Assigns Forever: The Life of Robert Shore, Minnesota Pioneer"
  (Unpublished, 1950).
Ideas Have Consequences: 125 Years of the Liberal Tradition in the Lansing Area (East
  Lansing, MI: Unitarian Universalist Church, 1973) (as Jerry Thornton).
Poems (East Lansing: MSU Department of American Thought and Language, 1975).
The Stone in My Pocket and Other Poems (East Lansing: Years Press/MSU
  Department of American Thought and Language, 1981).
"Football and Other Academic Arts at Michigan State University" (with Pauline G.
  Adams) (Paper delivered on May 6, 1982, at Annual Conference of the Society
  for the Study of Midwestern Literature).
A Populist Assault: Sarah E. Van De Vort Emery on American Democracy, 1862–1895
  (with Pauline Adams) (Bowling Green, IN: Bowling Green State University
  Popular Press, 1982).
Heart Songs of Nature (Ann Arbor: Bokmal Press, 2000).

Sites

. . . .

RAY STANNARD BAKER

Delta Street, East Lansing
Original Peoples Church site, approximately 105 East Grand River Avenue, East
  Lansing
Burial: Wildwood Cemetery, Amherst, Hampshire County, Massachusetts

EMMA SHORE THORNTON

Unitarian Universalist Church Memorial Garden, 855 Grove Street outside front
  entrance, East Lansing

Mary Frances Doner

Beyond Bodice Ripping

July 29, 1893–April 1, 1985

Born in Port Huron; attended school in Detroit and St. Clair; lived in Port Huron and Ludington

. . . .

Those old-time pulp writers never got the recognition they deserved.
—LOREN D. ESTLEMAN, *Infernal Angels*

Lake Huron rolls, so goes the Gordon Lightfoot lyric. Each wave breaking on its rocky Michigan shore tells a tale of its moiling journey and whether it brings happiness or heartache. Huron is the "sunrise side" according to a chamber of commerce slogan that suggests the dawn of a peaceably bright blue morning. It is also a graveyard of ships, according to the state historical marker on Michigan's northeast land's edge.

Mary Frances Doner was born in Port Huron, the town where the lake drains. Her father, a Marquette native, made his living from the lakes as ship captain and then as manager with the Reiss Steamship Company of Sheboygan, Wisconsin. From 1894 to 1910, the family lived in Detroit, where he captained the fire tug *Chief Battle*, named for the first chief of the nonvolunteer Detroit Fire Department. They next moved to St. Clair, where the father's absences from home proved trying; his young daughter coped with the separation by writing him long communiqués that dramatized

15

Mary Frances Doner, of Port Huron and Ludington, was the author of romances of the Great Lakes.

events with added imaginary details. Her father emended each letter, return-ing it with encouragement to be even more fanciful. According to one press clipping in her journals, she achieved publication before age ten when a friend of her mother's who dealt in fine ladies' material inspired her to write "my first story, about lace." It was "published in the company's house organ." When in port, Captain Doner took his daughter to the bridge aboard ship, where she became equally fascinated by the colorful conversation about events during the recent voyage and by the impressive controls.

Growing up in freshwater Port Huron, she fell in love with maritime lore and tradition. The town enjoys as much heritage as any place in Michigan. A French explorer landed in 1686, planting the first European flag and building a fort to impress the Ojibway, who have found the natural setting inspirational throughout their many generations. The American flag first flew at Fort Gratiot Lighthouse in 1825, the prototypical navigation aid in the state. Immediately prior to the Civil War, an enterprising young man named Edison sold newspapers on the train back and forth to Detroit. During that antebellum period, the town served as an Underground

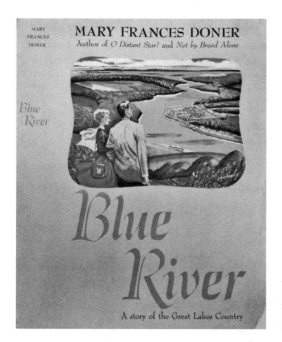

The cover of *Blue River*, Doner's novel set on the St. Clair River, epitomizes her subject matter.

Railroad terminus where escaped slaves, almost a stone's throw from Canada, crossed over to freedom. After the war, lumbering and ship building boomed. A couple of years before Mary's birth, the world's first international underwater railroad tunnel opened beneath the St. Clair River to connect Michigan to Sarnia, Ontario. The easternmost point in the state, today it is home to fourteen sites on the National Register of Historic Places and to seventeen Michigan historical markers. Her hometown overflows with history.

She attended school in Detroit before the family moved to St. Clair, where she graduated from high school. After moving to Cleveland, she married Elmer L. Moore, age thirty, a professional photographer, on January 2, 1915. Mary Frances—listing her name on the license as "Mamie F."—was twenty-one. By 1921 she resided in New York City, attending night classes at Columbia University and facing a key life decision.

Blanche Colton Williams headed up the short-story courses in the extension department at Columbia from 1914 until 1926. A writer of some stature, she served fourteen years as chair and first editor for the O. Henry Memorial

Prize, annual awards still being handed out for the best writing in that genre. Williams had thirty-five works credited to her as author or editor and "was for twenty-five years one of the busiest" people engaged in U.S. literary work.[1] Teaching at several schools, never married, she devoted herself to a career helping advance the writing talents of three thousand aspiring student authors—women especially.

One of her potential mentees was Mary Doner Moore. Along with her childhood fondness for writing, she had shown talent as a pianist. Which to choose—music or literary career? Williams encouraged her to choose letters, judging her writing to be "lovely and magnificent."

Mary Frances made her career decision. She began with the short-story form taught by Williams, submitting her first efforts to periodicals. Rejection letters, which she painstakingly maintained in a scrapbook as inspiration to persevere, were the response each time. Undaunted, she learned a simple antidote to failure: "work." In April 1922 the publisher of the *Cosmopolitan*, *Good Housekeeping*, and *Harper's Bazaar* magazines turned down a submission but with important counsel: yes, she could write, but she needed to "get out of theatrics and down to life." The advice was taken to heart. The next month found her notifying friends and parents that "Worlds Apart," a short story, would be published in *Illustrated Love Story* magazine. Captain and Mrs. Doner telegrammed to revel in the good news: "We are all very happy but not surprised hearty congratulations."

This first printed story was a romance. There is no category for the genre in the National Book Awards, just as the Pulitzer is never awarded for such an effort. Not until the 1980s would an association of authors, the Romance Writers of America, found its own set of awards and create a Hall of Fame.[2] Love stories began and would conclude her publishing career, the story lines following this basic arc: Kitty Kildare was an orphan. She grew up without much education and worked as a waitress—until she found rich great-uncle Owen. She had finally found a family and a place she could call home. Handsome Reed Chilvers was immediately taken with the pretty new girl in town. She was everything he wasn't. Kitty's easy generosity and frankness appealed to the prim and proper business executive. Kitty didn't think she was good enough for Reed. But Reed was determined to show her that their very different backgrounds didn't matter, at least to him.[3]

Romance became her raison d'être. By 1926 she was under contract with Dell Publishing Company for a romance novel of fifty thousand words, a story every other month for its magazine, and four short stories every other month of ten thousand words. She wasn't writing anonymously, for the contract specified use of a "pen name," Mary Frances Doner.

The return to her birth name signaled that the marriage had not endured. Seeking a fresh start, she moved to the Boston area in 1927, soon meeting a physician who was also a seascape painter of note. On January 8, 1930, she and Claude Payzant were married at the Pen and Brush Club in New York City. Her parents' hometown newspaper recounted the nuptials, noting that she was "well known as an authoress." Her notoriety and amiability gained her many friends in Boston social circles, and "Mimi" began writing for a Boston paper, convening literary luncheons, and corresponding with Michigan friends about her busy but now happy life.

Her first dozen books were published by the same houses that handled her serials: Chelsea House, Alfred H. King, and Penn Publishing. Penn issued a brochure about her books captioned "Romances of the Great Lakes." Her story "Curtain Call" appeared in the October 1937 *Real Charm* magazine along with pieces by Dorothy Parker and Edgar Lee Masters. Her articles caught the eye of editors at Doubleday, then the largest publisher in the United States and Great Britain, who signed her to their stable of writers. She would acknowledge it as her "big break." From then until 1952, Doubleday issued seven novels that gained her acclaim.

The new contract reflected a growing maturity in Doner's style. The pulp fiction she generated for so long had found favor with a mass audience; the genre has proved to be a storehouse of skill, exemplified in Sinclair Lewis, first American recipient of the Nobel Prize in Literature, who wrote and edited for *Adventure*, one of the most famous pulp magazines. Doner found it no longer enough. She challenged herself to refine the talent Williams had discovered: "I slowed down to writing 1,000 words a day, instead of 50,000 words a week, to earnestly strive for quality, instead of quantity." Setting the stories in the Great Lakes area also helped yield books of a more solid and lasting character.

Though residing in Boston, Doner returned to the region of her youth every summer to gather material for the next volume: "When I decide to do a book, I go where the action is."[4] Doner had her early Lake Huron days for background; she also had come to know heartbreak, two failed marriages (she and Payzant divorced in 1947, despite the 1938 *Gallant Traitor* dedication to "my husband and my friend"[5]), and the tragic death of her youngest brother, James, due to a ruptured appendix while on Christmas vacation from prep school. Memory and imagination provided the raw material; research while back in Michigan provided the substance. The July 1942 *Escanaba Daily Press* reported that she had been in town to investigate records at its office and the local Carnegie library. In her final Doubleday work, *The Host Rock*, Doner wrote of the search for uranium deposits in the Upper Peninsula as part of the frantic pace of the post–World War II nuclear arms race between the United States and the Soviet Union. To authenticate the story, she spent months at the Soo in Northern Michigan and in the countryside along the northeastern shore of Lake Superior. The *Port Huron Times Herald* bragged about how she "spends many hours at her typewriter in the reference rooms of Port Huron Public Library."

She located each of the Doubleday book settings in Michigan, filling them with richness beyond the early romance works. Not that these were altogether different in plot; they still followed a storyline heavy on melodrama. In her river-titled book, protagonist Anne Armour returns on Christmas Eve to the familiar hotel on the shore of the river that signified only heartbreak:

> She stood on the piazza in the almost paralyzing bitterness, looking down at Blue River. Under that ice it flowed—endomed yet living, breathing; a core of beauty, an indispensable link in these great waterways. Blue River, the one changeless thing in her life . . . It was not just a stream marking a boundary line and connecting the Great Lakes waterways. It was a friend who shared the happenings of her days. In the light of the rising sun its awesome wonder could almost still the beat of her heart, and with evening its proud gray face withdrew into a friendly eternity and made of darkness a promise rather than a mystery. . . . Anne would steal off to the willows near the shipyard. And the river would whisper back to her and straighten out the kinks in her heart.

Certain personal life experiences are echoed in this book. Anne plays piano exceptionally well. She knows Detroit. Several of the characters suffer from a major weakness of the soul. Society's prejudices and gossipy confidences flavor the story. Our heroine is not as pure as the ice on the river, it turns out, but she finds herself "the wife of one of Michigan's great men" as he builds an auto company. She learns that the great purpose of life is love—not merely an impulse or an emotion, but a sacrificial devotion to another. Difficult lessons are learned along "her river."

Blue River is a quintessentially modern Michigan book. Anne's husband builds a manufacturing plant and a planned city along the water, supplanting pastoral scenes in favor of profits. Instead of building a dream house, however, the couple renovate an old mansion on the river, hiring back the African American domestics for whom Brush Street in the Motor City was never as much a home as this place. Two strong women compete for the affection of one visionary businessman—both having as much character as he. In this prefeminist era, Doner gave her central figure many modern traits. Chief among them, though, is a classic characteristic for one romanticizing her home state: paramount adoration for her corner of Michigan.

Doner began extended visits to the west side of Michigan in 1952 when her brother, Edward Horace Doner, captain of the Lake Michigan car ferry to Wisconsin, was stationed at Ludington. Enchanted with the sunsets, she relocated to the port town in 1964. It, too, became a setting in her fiction.

By then, her publishing career was flickering out. A new passion took its place, carrying on the Williams legacy, teaching others how to write. In 1973 an enterprising reporter visited her Ludington home and took her measure: "Mary Frances blends with that strength-and-beauty setting—a gifted musician and writer—but also a practical hard-working gal with an Irish smile and an easy accommodation of life's quirky course." At eighty years of age, she still enjoyed writing—waking, getting breakfast, working the words until she became hungry sometime in early afternoon, leaving off in favor of research during the next hours until quitting for the day around four o'clock. Eventually, she had to give up her creative writing course at Ludington High School—a continuation of teaching done in Boston and Port Huron. A dozen bound volumes of course material remain in her collections at the Bentley Library in Ann Arbor.

Also in the Bentley material are confessions. One bound typewritten manuscript, "On Creative Writing," contains this:

The compulsive write because they have to, because the urge to write gives them no peace. They do not analyze the pressure—because it is beyond analysis. They do not pause to wonder. Rejection, discouragement, sacrifice are taken in stride. They do what they have to do . . . I am helpless in the vortex of creative thought, and of invention. I am driven, obsessed, pursued by the demands of the army of ideas that cry to be written.

Feeling her work had been only "modestly recognized and published," and that "I will never reach the heights dreamed of in the beginning," Doner nonetheless remained faithful to her career choice: "the dream has given my life texture and substance."

Some critics regarded her talent as middling, as in this *New York Times* review: "In spite of the earnestness of the author and her carefully documented background, both her character drawing and her story pattern seem as dated as the time in which they are placed." Movie studio MGM begged to differ. Doner signed a $5,000 contract for the rights to one book before publication (*Blue River*), which would have entitled her to another $25,000 had it been made into a motion picture. Some paid homage to Doner's writing, as in this review of *Not by Bread Alone* from the *Milwaukee Journal*:

This book could not be duplicated in another country. It is as American as a doughnut or a fountain pen. It is about some ordinary people in a little port on Lake Huron. Its theme is how they work through to success. By "success" understand "happiness." They do not achieve any appreciable amount of money. They do love each other.

A favorable review of O Distant Star! appeared in the Boston Sunday Post in February 1944:

When we reviewed her "Glass Mountain," about a year ago, we said that Mary Frances Doner rises a rung on the ladder of fame with every story she writes. But with "O Distant Star!" she skips all the intervening rungs, and lands at the very top. For this is one of the best American regional novels we have ever read. From childhood as a captain's daughter, Mary Frances has been steeped in Michigan history.

One fan, William W. Seward Jr., the head of the English Department at the College of William and Mary, wrote her in 1948 to obtain an autographed copy of *Ravenswood* because "the book is extremely well written. You have a way with words, you know what you are doing, and you tell a marvelous story. The characterizations, as well as the style, are most excellent." Since she had been included in a "New England Literary Tour" with Erskine Caldwell, John Dos Passos, and Kenneth Roberts, the professor was not merely daft.

Even the *New York Times* regarded her writing, in some cases, as well done. In 1942 its review of *Glass Mountain* judged it "a peculiarly American story made up of ingredients native to this soil . . . a warm, homespun tale . . . The book has the quality of an old-fashioned patchwork quilt, colorful and friendly and warm." The *Saturday Review of Literature* concurred: "The strength of the book is a warm and understanding portrait of [the main character] . . . She is fully drawn and real."

A Michigan newspaper, the *Marquette Daily Mining Journal* of November 23, 1942, best expressed the essence of her life's work: "Indubitably Mary Frances Doner has love of the lakes inbred in heart and bone, and she does well to make the Great Lakes the background for her novels." The *Boston Sunday Post* concurred: "Miss Doner has made the Great Lakes region of our country peculiarly her own, as far as fiction goes . . . Each of her novels has caught some of her affectionate feeling for that area." Perhaps the epitome is *Blue River*, a thinly disguised story about the St. Clair River, with a cover portraying the big stream winding down from a lake that must be Huron. Anchor Shores in the novel is Anchorville, Marineville is Marine City, and Little Venice is the St. Clair "Flats."

Her love for the water wonderland shows in the scrapbooks at the Bentley Library. They bear a custom front plate titled "Library of Mary Frances Doner," with an image of a lake and canoe occupied by a happy couple, within an opening of a forest, and above it a graphic portraying the outline of Michigan and the Great Lakes.[6] In a column for the *St. Clair County Press* she wrote of appearing on a panel at Albion College to discuss Michigan's literary resources for those interested in trying to write: "I argued that if one needs direction as to material with such magnificent inspiration at hand, then the mind must indeed be arid and the sense of observation dull." The dedication page to *Cloud of Arrows: The Story of a Woman's Strange Fidelity*[7] boasts: "The Michigan background is presented as authentically as possible by one who, since childhood, has loved the region where her forefathers were pioneers. M.F.D."

She loved it, then, because her parents and ancestors had first loved it. *Glass Mountain* began with a wistful dedication in the form of a poem, "To the Memory of My Father Captain James Doner":

Sometimes it seems, on a summer day,
As the breeze whips the river St. Clair,
That the *John P. Reiss* is ploughing by
With her first gallant master there.

Sometimes it seems along Huron's wild shore
That the Lake is almost as blue,
As it used to be in the days of yore
When I sailed those waters, too . . .

Sometimes it seems when spring comes round,
And the ice-floes plunge downstream,
That off on his season's jaunt he's bound
And the rest of it's only a dream.

When the sun sinks low and the twilight's soft
And the frogs make song in the brook,
A ghostly signal trembles aloft,
And down toward the river I look;

Where a shadow ship with a shadow mast
Sails on toward a harbor dim,
Where the ships of his mates are moored at last,
And wait for the coming of Jim . . .

Her final works, after the Doubleday relationship ended, included some history-related material and romances. She ended as she began, with melodrama. And on the Great Lakes.

Mary Frances Doner died on April 1, 1985, at the Baywood nursing home in Ludington where she had been a patient since 1981. Age ninety-one, she left behind an output of some 250 short stories and serials and thirty-one books. Her 1,500-volume library went to a Catholic home in Port Huron. Her remains were interred in Hillside Cemetery in St. Clair, near the bank of the Pine River before it empties into the watercourse she imaginatively called "the Suez Canal of the Great Lakes." Her writing may have been formulaic, like that of others who gain loyal and large readership, but through it all flowed a lifetime of stories based on the waters and people of Michigan.

Works

The Dancer in the Shadow: A Love Story (New York: Chelsea House, 1930).

The Lonely Heart: A Love Story (New York: Chelsea House, 1930).

The Dark Garden: A Love Story (New York: Chelsea House, 1930).

Broken Melody: A Love Story (New York: Chelsea House, 1932).

Fools' Heaven: A Love Story (New York: Chelsea House, 1932).

Forever More: A Love Story (New York: Chelsea House, 1934).

Let's Burn Our Bridges (New York: A.H. King, 1935).

Child of Conflict: A Love Story (New York: Chelsea House, 1936).

Gallant Traitor (Philadelphia: Penn Publishing, 1938).[8]

Some Fell among Thorns (Philadelphia: Penn Publishing, 1939).

Chalice (Philadelphia: Penn Publishing, 1940).[9]

The Doctor's Party (Philadelphia: Penn Publishing, 1940).

Not by Bread Alone (Garden City, NY: Doubleday, Doran, 1941).

Glass Mountain (Garden City, NY: Doubleday, Doran, 1942).

O Distant Star! (Garden City, NY: Doubleday, Doran, 1944).

Blue River: A Story of the Great Lakes Country (Garden City, NY: Doubleday, Doran, 1946).

Ravenswood: A Story of the Impact of a Family and an Industry on a Great Lakes Town (Garden City, NY: Doubleday & Co., 1948).

Cloud of Arrows: The Story of a Woman's Strange Fidelity (Garden City, NY: Doubleday & Co., 1950).

The Host Rock (Garden City, NY: Doubleday & Co., 1952).

The Salvager: The Life of Captain Tom Reid on the Great Lakes (Minneapolis: Ross and Haines, 1958).

While the River Flows—A Story of Life along the Great Lakes Waterways, of the Sailors and Their Loves (New York: Avalon Books, 1962).

The Shores of Home (New York: Thomas Bouregy & Co., 1961; New York: Airmont Books [Avalon], 1962).

The Wind and the Fog (New York: Thomas Bouregy & Co., 1962; New York: Avalon Books, 1963).

Cleavenger vs. Castle: A Case of Breach of Promise and Seduction (Philadelphia: Dorrance & Co., 1968).

The Old House Remembers (with Rose D. Hawley) (Ludington, MI: Lakeside Printing, 1968).

Pere Marquette—Soldier of the Cross (Ludington, MI: Pere Marquette Memorial Association, 1969).[10]

Return a Stranger (New York: Avalon Books, 1970).[11]

Thine Is the Power (New York: Avalon Books, 1972).

Not by Appointment (New York: Avalon Books, 1972).

The Darker Star (New York: Avalon Books, 1974).

Sites

402 Ninth Street and 615 North Third Street, St. Clair

1218 Washington Avenue, Port Huron

210 North Lewis Street, Ludington

Grave in Hillside Cemetery, in the city of St. Clair, on St. Clair Highway north of Palmer Street near the south city limits

Frances Margaret Fox

A Refuge for Children

June 23, 1870–March 1, 1959

Longtime resident of Bay City and Mackinaw City

· ·

Ideally, childhood is sheltered by the unconditional love of family and expressed through the unfettered exercise of the imagination. So there is grace when a child denied such love later in life tells stories of sweet youth to her young audience.

Frances Margaret Fox was born in South Framingham, Massachusetts. Her mother died two weeks after Frances's birth. Her father remarried and the family eventually moved to Mackinaw City, where he was a railroad dispatcher. Frances suffered at the hands of her father and stepmother. They beat her and reportedly sent her to a woodshed to sleep in a burlap hammock in cold weather.

She escaped in two ways. First, she delighted in the history and beauty of the Straits of Mackinac region, where she later set several of her children's stories. The lives of the Native Americans and the early French and English explorers and settlers captured her fancy. So, too, did the nearby great forests and abundant waters.

Frances Margaret Fox's difficult early childhood inspired her to write comforting, gentle, and instructive stories for a young audience. Courtesy of the Clarke Historical Library, Central Michigan University.

Second, in her teens, Frances was taken into the welcoming arms of a family that summered in the Straits area. She eventually moved to the Bay City home of attorney Lee Joslyn Sr. and became his secretary while tending to the Joslyn children, who became the first audience for her stories. Her tenderness bound them together for life.

Her sensitivity to vulnerable life of all forms was evident in her early volunteer work. She was identified as an associate editor of the *Bulletin of the Michigan Ornithological Society* in April 1897. Upon her enrollment in the society, the editor wrote, she "will aid us in her graceful writings to create and cultivate, among the thoughtless people of Michigan, a sentiment for the encouragement of our birds."

At twenty-eight, Fox began recording her stories and observations in a journal. On April 13, 1898, she wrote that she had invented a story about a tramp dog for young Lee Joslyn Jr. She sold it to a magazine two years later.

In her Mackinaw City home, Fox hosted children for storytelling time. She dubbed the house Happy Landings. Courtesy of Sandy Planisek.

The same year that story appeared in print, she published her first book, *Farmer Brown and the Birds*. It was the beginning of a prolific career. In the next forty-six years she authored fifty-two books and numerous stories for children's magazines.

Her annual routine was consistent. She spent summers in Mackinaw City and the cold months in Washington, D.C., researching her subjects—the behavior of toads, for example, or the founding of Detroit. She wanted to get it right, making her animals behave realistically and making her recounting of history unimpeachable.

She won the trust of the staff of the Library of Congress, becoming one of the few allowed access to the stacks. She spent considerable time at the Smithsonian Institution and told a story on herself. Wrote a reporter: "Instructed by an attendant to go through a door marked 'no admittance' to find an employee with whom she wished to confer, she blithely walked through the doorway into a room alive with small (harmless, she hoped) snakes and other reptiles. She admitted she cut her studies a little short thereafter."

Her writing success made it possible for her to build two successive houses in Mackinaw City, the latter of which was a stone structure made of locally quarried rock and facing the Straits. She dubbed it Happy Landings. She invited neighborhood children over for stories and refreshments. This informal band was known as the Sunshine Club. Frances tried out some of her stories on the children before sending them to her publisher.

Her Little Bear series was characteristic. Little Bear appears in twelve books, the first published in 1915. The books were intended for third and fourth graders. He is a sweet innocent, whose only faults may be naïveté and the mind of a dreamer. Little Bear learns and heeds the lessons his parents teach him.

In *Little Bear at Work and at Play*, a collection of stories previously published in *Youth's Companion* and the *Christian Observer*, the happy little central character accumulates life wisdom while learning to swim, enjoying a surprise party, and understanding the importance of work.

Humility is the lesson taught in "When Little Bear Bragged." Passing a rainy day in the family's house in the woods, Father Bear and Mother Bear take turns telling stories while Little Bear listens. Mother Bear recounts the classic story of the tortoise and the hare. Little Bear mocks the hare for being foolish enough to take a nap and lose the race.

"Wasn't he silly!" says Little Bear. "If I were going to run a race with Grandpa Tortoise, I should go this way until I reached the goal!"

Father Bear takes note of the little one's overconfidence and arranges a race between Little Bear and Grandpa Tortoise. Bounding off with self-assurance, Little Bear is distracted when Friend Treetoad offers him a cup of dew. He wants to drink from a spring. Beside the spring are frogs who ask him to play. He obliges. Suddenly baby rabbits appear. Little Bear can't resist playing with them and the squirrels. An hour passes before Little Bear realizes he's supposed to be running a race. But by the time he reaches the finish line, Grandpa Tortoise has won.

It turns out that Father Bear had sent the baby rabbits to test his son. Chastened, Little Bear remembers his manners and shakes Grandpa Tortoise's hand. Back home, the storytelling resumes. "Little Bear asked a few questions, as usual, that afternoon when the stories were told, but he did not brag."

Frances also wrote books for older children. Many of these were adventures set in the Mackinac region, such as *Little Mossback Amelia*, based on the true story of a pioneer girl growing up near what is now Petoskey. Another is *Uncle Sam's Animals*, which tells of wildlife protected by the government, such as Alaskan seals and wolves.

What Gladys Saw is a tale of a city girl gone to the country who studies nature under the supervision of wise elders. *Outlook* magazine said it was "told with as much picturesqueness as truth, and will surely delight other young people."

An example of fiction she set in the Straits area, *Ellen Jane* is about a young girl whose family lives for a summer in the McGulpin Point Lighthouse, which remains a tourist attraction today. Ellen Jane comes to love the beauty of the local woods and waters.

Fox had been educated at the Kalamazoo Seminary, and a strong religious faith underlay her writing. Of *Legend of the Christ Child*, a reader wrote, "She does not forget to remind the children that [the characters] are legends; but she manages, effortlessly, to convey the truth, that all creation rejoiced when the Child was born in Bethlehem."

Frances's art was a direct reaction to her childhood. She had "an inflexible rule that only happiness and gaiety must appear in her books for children," wrote a *Bay City Times* reporter who caught up with her in 1946. "I had to kill one small boy, a character in an early book," she said, "and it took a week's vacation for me to get over it. However I simply couldn't tell the story any other way." She did not repeat this story line.

She permitted no shadow of her childhood to darken her demeanor. "Her elfin smile and the pixie quality of her humor and philosophy make her popular with Bay City friends, who entertain her merrily on weekends and holidays," the reporter added. After her death she was remembered as "a tiny dark-haired woman with a wonderful smile and a good word for everyone." There may have been an unconscious message in her story-writing philosophy. "I never look backward. I'm only interested in the next book."

A clue to her philosophy of the treatment of children came as her writing career began, when she penned an essay published in the proceedings of the 1898 annual convention of the Michigan State Board of Corrections and Charities. "I believe that a little boy is more benefited by the gift of a ten-cent tin engine which will amuse him for hours and give him an opportunity to be several different imaginary persons whose services he must perform than a ten-cent handkerchief, which is one of the so-called useful presents."

She went on to declare, "Children are good . . . To be perfectly fair and true in all our dealings with all the children would preserve in them their inborn faith in the purity and good intentions of the world about them." To be otherwise could drive children down the road toward misbehavior or worse, she suggested. The essay prompted several delegates at the convention to say they were moved and reminded of the sadness of sending a child to a reformatory.

Frances was a minor celebrity in her hometown. The city council asked her to rename Mackinaw City's streets. Steeped in local history, she chose names of the area's early French and British traders and soldiers—Jamet, DuCharme, Longlade, Sinclair, and Henry. Received politely by state authorities, her suggestion that the city be renamed Michilimackinac was unsuccessful.

After World War II, her production ceased. Frances passed away in a Detroit retirement home. But true home was always Mackinaw City. She had asked to be cremated and to have her ashes strewn in her beloved Straits of Mackinac. Alan Joslyn, one of the children on whom she had tested her first stories, honored her final wish.

Works

Farmer Brown and the Birds (Boston: L.C. Page and Co., 1900).

Betty of Old Mackinaw (Boston: L.C. Page and Co., 1901).

What Gladys Saw: A Nature Story of Farm and Forest (Boston: W.A. Wilde Co., 1902).

Little Lady Marjorie (Boston: L.C. Page and Co., 1903).

The Little Giant's Neighbors (Boston: L.C. Page and Co., 1903).

Mother Nature's Little Ones (Boston: L.C. Page and Co., 1903).

How Christmas Came to the Mulvaneys (Boston: L.C. Page and Co., 1905).

The Rainbow Bridge: A Story (Boston: L.C. Page and Co., 1905).

The Country Christmas (Boston: L.C. Page and Co., 1907).

Brother Billy (Boston: L.C. Page and Co., 1908).

Carlota: A Story of the San Gabriel Mission (Boston: L.C. Page and Co., 1908).

Seven Christmas Candles (Boston: L.C. Page and Co., 1909).

Seven Little Wise Men (Boston: L.C. Page and Co., 1910).

Mary Anne's Little Indian: And Other True Stories for Children (Chicago: A. Flanagan, 1913).

Doings of Little Bear (Chicago: Rand McNally and Co., 1915).

Adventures of Sonny Bear (Chicago: Rand McNally and Co., 1916).

The Adventures of Blackberry Bear (New York: Moffat, Yard and Co., 1918).

The Kinderkins (Chicago: Rand McNally and Co., 1918).

Little Bear at Work and at Play (Chicago: Rand McNally and Co., 1920).

Little Bear's Playtime (Chicago: Rand McNally and Co., 1922).

Little Bear's Adventures (New York: Rand McNally and Co., 1923).

Ellen Jane (New York: Rand McNally and Co., 1924).

Little Bear Stories (New York: Rand McNally and Co., 1924).

Little Bear's Laughing Times (New York: Rand McNally and Co., 1924).

Nan's Christmas Boarder (Boston: L.C. Page, 1924).

Little Bear's Ups and Downs (Chicago: Rand McNally and Co., 1925).

Janey (Chicago: Rand McNally and Co., 1925).

Sister Sally (Chicago: Rand McNally and Co., 1925).

Janey Seeking a Home (Chicago: Rand McNally and Co., 1926).

Angeline Goes Traveling (New York: Rand McNally and Co., 1927).

Uncle Sam's Animals (New York: Century Co., 1927).

Little Bear's Ins and Outs (New York: Rand McNally and Co., 1928).

Ellen Jane (Chicago: Rand McNally and Co., 1928).

Nancy Davenport (Chicago: Rand McNally and Co., 1928).

Nannette (New York: P.F. Volland Co., 1929).

The Wildling Princess (Joliet, IL: P.F. Volland Co., 1929).

Washington, D.C.: The Nation's Capital; Romance, Adventure, Achievement; A Book for Young People (Chicago: Rand McNally, 1929).

Mary Anne's Little Indian and Other True Stories (Chicago: A. Flanagan Co., 1930).

The Magic Canoe: A Frontier Story of the American Revolution (Chicago: Laidlaw Brothers, 1930).

Adventures of Sonny Bear (Chicago: Rand McNally and Co., 1934).

Stories for Little Brother and Sister (Akron, OH: Saalfield Publishing Co., 1936).

Flowers and Their Travels (Indianapolis: Bobbs and Merrill, 1936).

Little Toad (New York: Viking Press, 1938).

Little Mossback Amelia (New York: E.P. Dutton, 1939).

They Sailed and Sailed (New York: E.P. Dutton, 1940).

Legend of the Christ Child (New York: Sheed and Ward, 1941).

Quakers Courageous (Boston: Lothrop, Lee and Shepard Co., 1941).

True Monkey Stories (Boston: Lothrop, Lee and Shepard Co., 1941).

Gay Legends of the Saints (New York: Sheed and Ward, 1942).

Sites

Home, 512 N. Huron, Mackinaw City

McGulpin Point Lighthouse and Historic Site, 500 Headlands Road, Mackinaw City

Joslyn Home, 815 Fifth Street, Bay City

Donald Joseph Goines

A Graphic Life

December 15, 1938–October 21, 1974
Born, lived, and died in Detroit

The mean streets of inner city Detroit are legendary, having labored hard
to earn the reputation. Addiction and associated criminal activity are
altogether too common. Employing such dark personal experiences as an
integral part of one's craft—to ensuing popular patronage—is a distinction
worthy of scrutiny.

Donald Goines wrote sixteen uncompromisingly gritty novels arising from those grim avenues. He won no award, but his writing found an
audience that endures forty years after his epic demise at the hands of an
unknown gunman. His prodigious output was fueled by pharmaceuti-
cals no medical condition required, no doctor prescribed. Perhaps critics
should scorn his popularity and deride any serious literary stature; after all,
great writers should need no artificial aids.

Relegate Goines, then, to the category of other moral failures: Oscar
Wilde (opium), Robert Louis Stevenson (cocaine), Carl Sagan (marijuana),
William S. Burroughs (heroin), and Philip K. Dick (amphetamines). Ignore

Goines attended Elizabeth Cleveland Intermediate School, a Donaldson and Meier design featuring an inspirational library; it became a charter academy.

that five of the first seven American-born writers awarded the Nobel Prize for Literature—Sinclair Lewis, Eugene O'Neill, William Faulkner, Ernest Hemingway, and John Steinbeck—confronted the tribulations of alcohol dependency. A national news outlet began a profile in this fashion:

> The literary work of Donald Goines probably receives little if any attention in literature courses and book clubs around the country, yet the Detroit-born story-teller sold well over 5 million novels during his life, a life plagued by drug addiction and prison time.[1]

In a lifetime of less than forty years, with only five years spent compiling his body of work, it just might be that his African descent, Native American blood, educational shortcomings, and urban realism cost him a chance at immortality. Despite these attributes—perhaps due to them—he shared a trait with the coterie above. He could write.

Goines attended kindergarten at Sacred Heart Church on Detroit's east side. The Ren Cen symbolized hopes for a better future after the city's racial conflicts of the 1960s.

Born in Depression-era Detroit, Goines was the son of small-business owners who achieved some success despite general and local economic obstacles. His birth to African Americans, fifty-year-old father Joseph and much younger and lighter-skinned mother Myrtle, brought the blessing of a large circle of relations. The family lived on the east side of the city, and Donald began attending kindergarten at Sacred Heart Catholic School on Eliot at Rivard, near the Eastern Market. After many of the founding German parishioners left, the first black Catholic congregation in the city moved to the area in 1938. His father spent most hours at the family dry-cleaning store, boosting his fortunes through hard work and taxing them by partying in off-hours. Early in childhood, Donald accompanied his dad to a bar on Dequindre, witnessing poker marathons and prodigious bouts of beer drinking.

In January 1946, shifting family economics required "Donnie" to become a public school brat at nearby Davison Elementary. The family had moved to a house near Davison and Dequindre, where they opened a new dry-cleaning shop. He next attended Elizabeth Cleveland Intermediate, a lanky and imposing structure designed by the renowned Detroit architecture firm of Donaldson and Meier. Incorporating a hallway that ran the length of the building, it also featured a beautiful library with wood paneling, arched doorways, a fireplace, and bay window. Though his environs could have inspired pursuit of excellence, Donnie did not focus on his studies.

All three of the Goines children—Donnie, older sister Marie, and younger sister Joan (born in 1948)—were expected to help keep the store humming. In his free time, he played baseball with skill, but family rarely attended a game. He tried to be dutiful; he attended Mass and volunteered to drive the nuns to their retreats outside the city. Entering Pershing High School in 1951, he was drawn to the streets of the east side, near the Brewster Project and Frederick Douglass Apartments, Black Bottom, Hastings Street, and the primarily black neighborhoods on that side of Woodward Avenue. Establishment Detroit neglected this community; the city's population was at its apogee, a new civic center would rise on Jefferson at Woodward, more highways would fill trenches carved into lower-class neighborhoods, and misplaced pride and official neglect would contribute to undermining the fragile economy that African Americans had built for themselves.

Teenage Goines was drawn to the drama and excitement of tough streets. Though his father sought to rescue a budding delinquent by constructing a recreation room on the second floor above the cleaners for son and friends, Goines instead used it to engage in minor criminal hijinks. Eventually realizing the trajectory he was on, at age fifteen he took Marie's birth certificate, altered it into his own—with a birth date in 1934—and joined the U.S. Air Force in 1952.

While he was stationed in Japan, military life subjected Goines to racial discrimination he had not directly experienced back home. Integration of the armed services had begun, but attitudes did not change overnight. Goines had difficulties with discipline, even though for a time he served as a military police officer. He had no challenge consuming an ever-increasing diet of substances, beginning with marijuana, and moving into hashish, opium, and finally heroin. Discharged after his term was up at age seventeen, he returned to Detroit in 1955 as a different kind of veteran.

Though his father had hopes, the returning soldier had no intention of taking over the family business. He worked as a truck driver, on an auto assembly line, and then as a pimp. He sired five children with three women. In January 1961, he and two sidekicks robbed a numbers establishment at gunpoint. Apprehended and convicted, Goines was sent to the state penitentiary at Jackson. Soon out on parole, he was convicted of bootlegging in August 1965 in the courtroom of federal jurist Wade H. McCree Jr. and was sent away again, this time to the federal prison in Terre Haute, Indiana.

Goines was released in 1968, but was sent back to Jackson the next year for attempted larceny. On a prison visit, a relative brought a typewriter so that he could write letters to the family. The timing could not have been better. Goines had just become enamored of a black writer known as Iceberg Slim. His legal name was Robert Beck, and his life paralleled Goines's in some major ways: pimping, extended time in the joint, a talent for writing. Slim's fictional autobiography, *Pimp: The Story of My Life*, fascinated Goines and gave him the idea of seriously trying some creative writing of his own. Rather than type his story, Donald handwrote on reams of loose-leaf paper. It was authentic, based on his Detroit street experiences. Audaciously, he sent it to the Los Angeles publishing house that had issued Beck's first and subsequent books, Holloway House.

The flier paid off. Two weeks before his release in December 1970, Goines signed a contract with Holloway to publish *Whoreson*, the manuscript he had labored on in the Big House. Arriving at the family home on Maine Street in eastside Detroit, he immediately began work on his next book, titling it *Dopefiend*. For this he received an advance of $750. He soon followed up with a third book, *Black Gangster*, and attracted a female companion, Shirley Ann Sailor, ten years his junior, who already had two children. The couple had a child and moved to Los Angeles, where Goines got a bit part in the Charlton Heston film *Soylent Green*. He had come a long way rapidly.

He brought along his habit. While churning out novel upon novel, Goines continued to employ heroin. He felt it was essential to the flow of his creativity, allowing him to keep up a frantic pace: "If I get a shot of heroin, I'm able to work from morning to night, my writing seems to be better, and I can think." He made money, spent it, made more, gambled it away, made yet more, and blew it on smack. "I want to write," he affirmed, but he felt compelled to turn out work "like comic books."[2] Success did not prevent self-loathing; at one point he wrote, "Being of the black race, there is always the chance that we will contaminate whatever we touch."

He was not without virtues. He had warned his younger sister away from drugs. He was faithful to Shirley. He had sought to create a domestic haven for the children, hers and theirs. They decided to leave Los Angeles and drive to Detroit, found a house in Highland Park, and sought a more secure life. Goines continued to pump out books about pushers and pimps. He wrote under his own name and the pseudonym Al C. Clark, derived from the name of a good friend. The latter approach enabled two of his books to be in the market at the same time without compromising sales. He also continued to use, and the money continued to come in and fly out.

In May 1974, Goines made out a will. He assigned the royalties from each book to one of his children or another family member. He had one requirement for the inheritance to vest: they had to go by his last name; if not, the bequest passed to the others. For once, family pride flourished.

After sixteen books, and still no wealthier than when his first appeared, Goines noted with foreboding in a journal that "I have to work fast." On October 21, just six months after authoring his testament, Goines and Sailor were the victims of unknown assailants in their Cortland Street house. The perpetrators were never apprehended. A story in the next day's newspaper failed to mention that Goines was an author. His death was covered along with other murders in Highland Park that ordinary day, as if he was just one more typical urban casualty. His older sister ensured that his death certificate listed "writer" as the deceased's occupation. Someone had to memorialize his talent.

In 1990, as hip-hop began making its impact felt around America, a reference to Goines appeared in a song by an artist named Brand Nubian. The subject matter of his books fit well the earthy urban themes embodied by the rap genre, and some critics credit Goines with fathering this type of music. In 2004, the noir film *Never Die Alone* debuted, based on Goines's book of that title, with rapper/actor DMX (Earl Simmons) in the starring role. Famed film critic Roger Ebert awarded it three-and-a-half out of four stars, calling it much more than just another crime and drugs story, showcasing "the complexity of serious fiction and the nerve to start dark and stay dark, to follow the logic of its story right down to its inevitable end."

Ebert could have been summarizing Goines's abbreviated life. His grave, among the Detroit Memorial Park possibilities, lacks an appropriate headstone. His work, though, has not faded away. Publisher Holloway House in Los Angeles, on Melrose Avenue close by the Sunset Strip, kept him in print for the next three decades and beyond before selling its assets in 2008. The new owner, New York publishing house Kensington, calls Goines "the godfather of urban lit." His book covers underline the author's stature as "America's #1 Best Selling Black Author." Academia has taken notice. One professor credits him as having "established the conventions and the popular momentum for a new fictional genre, which could be called ghetto realism."[3] To another critic, Goines's novels "are written from ground zero."[4] Something is attracting a continuing readership, for one answer to the question "who's reading his books?" is that "primarily there are newer generations of young folks."[5]

Do they find much of the noble? The language is rough, scatological, rife with street slang. His heroes are flawed, life is tragic, and love is scarce; when it is found, there are few happy endings. The climax of *Black Girl Lost* is emblematic:

Sandra knew that the policemen were in the living room. She glanced down at Chink. She could see the fear in his eyes as he stared up into her face. She leaned down and kissed him, and as she held him close he tried to put his arms around her, but it took too much of his strength. He dropped his arms back on the bed.

When Sandra finished kissing him, she raised up suddenly. The knife she kept concealed in her pants outfit flashed once in the afternoon sunlight as she brought it down quickly. . . ." You don't ever have to worry about them lockin' you up no more, Daddy," she said quietly and let the knife drop from her hand. She leaned over and began to sob, and when the bedroom door flew open she didn't even bother to glance up.

The two officers entered the room cautiously. They watched the couple on the bed warily. The sight was one that neither man would ever forget.

Sandra neither glanced up at the men nor acknowledged them. She continued to lie at the side of her man, crying deep sobs that seemed to come from the bottom of her soul. . . . Her grief was hers and hers alone. Whether she was tried for his death or not didn't make any difference to her now. All that mattered was that her man was free.

He was free at last.

This is a kind of black experience with its own civil rights struggle.

English author and bon vivant Beverley Nichols could not have led a life more different from Goines's. His musing on the lost grave of a departed soul is, nonetheless, a fitting epitaph for the writer from Detroit:

> I don't know where his ashes lie, but presumably they lie somewhere. And if you believe, as I do, that in all ashes there is the germ of life, if you share my fancy that every grave, however remote or obscure, is never quite deserted, and that even if the grasses have grown thick around it, they sometimes bear the print of visiting footsteps, however faint or humble . . . then maybe you will hope with me that somewhere, far away, these words may bring a little glow to a handful of dust. It must be pleasant, I think, to be kindly spoken of, even after one is dead.[6]

The street justice that Donald Goines wrote about became the coda to his rough life. Whether he received justice as a literary figure is questionable. Like the city where he was born and died, he made choices that redounded to his detriment. Like that city, his reputation has not kept pace with his art.

Works

Dopefiend: The Story of a Black Junkie (Los Angeles: Holloway House, 1971).

Whoreson: The Story of a Ghetto Pimp (Los Angeles: Holloway House, 1972).

Black Gangster (Los Angeles: Holloway House, 1972).

Street Players (Los Angeles: Holloway House, 1973).

White Man's Justice, Black Man's Grief (Los Angeles: Holloway House, 1973).

Black Girl Lost (Los Angeles: Holloway House, 1973).

Crime Partners (as Al C. Clark, Kenyatta series) (Los Angeles: Holloway House, 1974).

Cry Revenge! (Los Angeles: Holloway House, 1974).

Daddy Cool (Los Angeles: Holloway House, 1974).

Death List (as Al C. Clark, Kenyatta series) (Los Angeles: Holloway House, 1974).

Eldorado Red (Los Angeles: Holloway House, 1974).

Kenyatta's Escape (as Al C. Clark, Kenyatta series) (Los Angeles: Holloway House, 1974).

Never Die Alone (Los Angeles: Holloway House, 1974).

Swamp Man (Los Angeles: Holloway House, 1974).

Inner City Hoodlum (Los Angeles: Holloway House, 1975).

Kenyatta's Last Hit (as Al C. Clark, Kenyatta series) (Los Angeles: Holloway House, 1975).

Sites

13953 St. Aubin Street, Detroit

13224 Dequindre Street, Detroit

17186 Maine Street, Detroit

232 Cortland Street, Highland Park

Sacred Heart School, Eliot at Rivard, Detroit

Davison Elementary School, 2800 East Davison Service Drive, Detroit

Elizabeth Cleveland Intermediate School, Conant at Charles Street, Detroit

John J. Pershing High School, 18875 Ryan Road, Detroit

Ernest Miller Hemingway

Man and Nature

July 21, 1899–July 2, 1961

Summer cottage on Walloon Lake; regular visitor to environs and Upper Peninsula

Out through the front of the tent he watched the glow of the fire, when the night wind blew on it. It was a quiet night. The swamp was perfectly quiet. Nick stretched under the blanket comfortably.—ERNEST HEMINGWAY, "Big Two-Hearted River, Part One"

At the far southwest end of Lake Michigan is a metropolis with a character unlike that of anything at the far north end of the same lake. A great body of water is all the two seem to have in common. A century ago, the difference was even starker. But one talent united them—the life and writing of the young Ernest Hemingway.

The second child of a successful physician, Ernest Miller Hemingway was born in Oak Park, Illinois, a middle-class suburb whose restrained style distinguished it from the brawling City of Big Shoulders about ten miles east. He was raised, according to the Hemingway Resource Center, "with the conservative Midwestern values of strong religion, hard work, physical fitness and self determination," a supposedly immutable creed that would be shattered by a face-to-face meeting with the horrors of a world war.

Even before this transformation—and his own—in the forge of armed conflict, Ernest found both comfort and human complications in a resort setting frequented by his parents in northern Michigan. His parents took Ernest and his siblings to a cooler, quieter habitat: first via steamer to Harbor Springs on Little Traverse Bay; then by train to Petoskey along a right of way that now serves as one of Michigan's most spectacular bike trails; and finally by rowboat to the family cottage.

At a summer house called Windemere on Walloon Lake, only a few miles from the big lake, he spent nineteen summers by the time he turned twenty-one, learning to fish, hunt, and observe. The observations became the clay Hemingway sculpted into more than a half-dozen stories from a larger, loosely connected series featuring a protagonist not unlike the young Ernest, named Nick Adams. The northern Michigan tales capture a human society of intrigue, love, courage, cowardice, and prejudice set before the mute grandeur of lakes, forests, fish, and wildlife—the ingredients of what he would define as a man's life.

Ernest's first visit to what would become Windemere took place when he was six weeks old. On that trip his parents selected the site of the cottage. The $400 structure contained a small kitchen, two bedrooms, and window seats on either side of the fireplace that also served as beds for Ernest and his older sister. The small original structure of Windemere was altered and expanded. The Hemingways added a kitchen wing and a screened porch, often used for meals. They added a three-bedroom sleeping annex behind the cottage as the number of children increased to six. A boathouse safely stored the canoe and boats in the off-season.

At first, Ernest's up-north life centered on Windemere. As he grew older, Ernest often rowed across Walloon Lake and hiked several miles to the village of Horton's Bay. He felt fond enough of it to marry his first wife, Hadley Richardson, there on September 2, 1921. They were wed in a Methodist church and walked across the road to the reception. They rode in a Model T Ford to Walloon Lake. Ernest rowed them across the lake to Windemere. They spent their honeymoon at the cottage.

During Hemingway's youth, a northern Michigan economy once powered by industrial, even rapacious logging was yielding to one based on the lure of its natural beauty for tourists. The slash and desolation of the cutover

Ernest Hemingway turned the majesty of northern Michigan into a stage for his immortal Nick Adams stories.

country slowly gave way to second-growth forest under the careful ministrations of public forestry champions. Something of the haunting glory of the region's primeval past reemerged to filter through the woods like moonlight. And something of both a distant past and a disorienting early twentieth-century present breathes in the stories this setting helped inspire.

The Nick Adams stories roughly parallel young Ernest's life. The first pieces portray Nick as a child of six, innocent but awakening; others describe an adolescent exploring pleasures and suffering trials. Several trace the experiences of a young man at war; the final stories powerfully and simply tell the struggle of a veteran, still young, to reclaim himself in the woods and streams of the Upper Peninsula.

Not all of the northern Michigan stories are Nick Adams tales. In one of them, "Up in Michigan," featuring a character named Jim Gilmore, Hemingway scandalized a publisher and members of his own family with a chronicle of young romance and lust. A sister called it a "vulgar, sordid tale." The story's raw denouement with Jim and Liz Coates on a dock has excited distaste, approbation, and deep critique since its publication in 1923.

Hemingway volunteered as an ambulance driver and served at the European front during World War I. He sustained serious wounds and recuperated for months in hospitals. Like many war veterans, he found his psychic wounds took longer to heal; they may never have done so. The experience of battle and its aftereffects on body and soul are among his central themes.

Perhaps the most moving of the Nick Adams stories is "Big Two-Hearted River," modeled after the nearby Fox River. After returning from war a hollowed-out man, Nick travels by train to Seney in the eastern Upper Peninsula, disembarks, and tramps through country recently ravaged by fire—not unlike the ruins of a battlefield. The close-up, small details of nature—a stream swirling with trout, a kingfisher, a grasshopper—capture his attention. As the hours pass, his spirit gradually renews. Detached from human company, Nick finds a growing contentment in a simple camp and hours of fishing. The style of prose for which Hemingway is famous photographs—or paints—a place in time.

If there is any doubt of the influence of northern Michigan landscapes in forming Hemingway's writing aesthetic, this deleted passage from "Big Two-Hearted River" dispels it:

> He, Nick, wanted to write about country so it would be there like Cezanne had done it in painting. You had to do it from inside yourself . . . He felt almost holy about it. It was deadly serious. You could do it if you would fight it out. If you'd lived right with your eyes. It was a thing you couldn't talk about . . . He knew just how Cezanne would paint this stretch of river.

Of this story, published in the collection *In Our Time*, critic Edmund Wilson said: "Out of the colloquial American speech, with its simple declarative sentences and its strings of Nordic monosyllables, he got effects of the utmost subtlety." But, Wilson added, "the European sensibility . . . has come to Big Two Hearted River, where the Indians are now obsolescent; in those solitudes it feels for the first time the cold current, the hot morning sun, sees the pine stumps, smells the sweet fern. And along with the mottled trout, with its 'clear water-over-gravel color,' the boy from the American Middle West brings up a fat little masterpiece."

In a 1919 letter to a friend, Hemingway described his attachment to northern Michigan in words Nick Adams might have used. "It is great northern air. Absolutely the best trout fishing in the country. No exaggeration. Fine country. Good color, good northern atmosphere, absolute freedom, no summer resort stuff and lots of paintable stuff. And it is equally good to run over to the Pine Barrens where it is absolutely wild and there are The Big and Little Sturgeon and Minnehaha and Black Trout Rivers. It's a great place to laze around and swim and fish when you want to. And the best place in the world to do nothing. It is beautiful country Jim."

After World War I, Hemingway became (in the long run) perhaps the most famous of a colony of American expatriates, many of them artists, in Paris. There he met up with F. Scott Fitzgerald, John Dos Passos, and others. His acclaimed work began with publication of *The Sun Also Rises* in 1926, followed by *A Farewell to Arms*, based on his war experiences, in 1929.

After 1921, Hemingway rarely returned to northern Michigan. In 1957, he brought his fourth wife, Mary, to view his family's cottage and the world in which he spent the summers of his youth. But by then he had long since belonged to a bigger world.

Even though he wrote none of his novels or the Nick Adams stories in Michigan, it is clear that the northern Michigan settings that shaped Hemingway also shaped some of his recurrent themes, and that their geography remained fixed in his imagination. Correspondent James Barron of the *New York Times* wrote in 1985: "Later in life Hemingway wanted people to think that his place was at bullfights in Spain, at cafes in Paris or on safaris in Africa. But he never really erased the map of northern Michigan from his mind. As he saw it, northern Michigan was a rough world of old loggers' camps and Indians, fishing and hunting, and freight trains rumbling distantly through the night."

In one of the early Nick Adams tales, "Indian Camp," the young Nick attends childbirth with his physician father. As the Native American mother screams with the pain of a torturous delivery, her husband slits his throat. At story's end, Nick rows with his father back across the lake:

"Do many men kill themselves, Daddy?"
  "Not very many, Nick."
  "Is dying hard, Daddy?"
  "No, I think it's pretty easy, Nick. It all depends."

Hemingway received the 1954 Nobel Prize for Literature, the prize committee citing his "mastery of the art of narrative, most recently demonstrated in *The Old Man and the Sea*, and for the influence that he has exerted on contemporary style." Somewhat uncharacteristically, the author told the press that Carl Sandburg, Isak Dinesen, and Bernard Berenson deserved the prize in his stead—but that he appreciated the prize money.

Melancholy can be traced through the Hemingway generations. Ernest's father took his own life in 1929, a sister in 1966, his only brother in 1982, and his granddaughter Margaux in 1996. Ernest became increasingly disturbed in the late 1950s, and his illness only worsened after electroshock therapy at the Mayo Clinic in late 1960. Depressed about his physical infirmities and the draining of his creative powers, Ernest shot himself in his Sun Valley, Idaho, home in 1961.

Today much of northern Michigan's Hemingway country survives, and so do structures that had meaning in his life. Windemere stands beside Walloon Lake. Privately owned and closed to the public, it is listed on both the State and National Register of Historic Places. The Horton Bay General Store, described in "Up in Michigan," attracts tourists on the Charlevoix-Boyne City Road. The nearly 135-year-old store is still a hub of business and social life in the village. Hemingway frequently visited the store, and Hemingway photos and memorabilia are displayed there. Beside the store is the Red Fox Inn, converted to a restaurant in 1919, and now home to a bookstore that specializes in Hemingway titles and memorabilia. Horton Creek, in which Hemingway fished, and Walloon Lake, of course, remain.

Although Hemingway's literary reputation waxes and wanes over the years, he is such a seminal influence that fans celebrated his 1999 centenary not only in Michigan but also in Florida, Idaho, Arkansas, Massachusetts, and Illinois, as well as Cuba, Italy, France, Spain, China, and Japan.

What also stands after all the years is the lucid beauty of his prose, the still-unspoiled settings of his northern Michigan stories, and the natural world that challenged and comforted him.

Works

NOVELS

The Torrents of Spring (New York: Scribner's, 1926).

The Sun Also Rises (New York: Scribner's, 1926).

A Farewell to Arms (New York: Scribner's, 1929).

To Have and Have Not (New York: Scribner's, 1937).

For Whom the Bell Tolls (New York: Scribner's, 1940).

Across the River and into the Trees (New York: Scribner's, 1950).

The Old Man and the Sea (New York: Scribner's, 1952).

Islands in the Stream (New York: Scribner's, 1970).

The Garden of Eden (New York: Scribner's, 1986).

True at First Light (New York: Scribner's, 1999).

COLLECTIONS

Three Stories and Ten Poems (Paris: Contact Publishing, 1923).

In Our Time (New York: Boni & Liveright, 1925).

Men without Women (New York: Scribner's, 1927).

Winner Take Nothing (New York: Scribner's, 1933).

The Fifth Column and the First Forty-Nine Stories (New York: Scribner's, 1938).

The Snows of Kilimanjaro and Other Stories (New York: Scribner's, 1961).

The Fifth Column and Four Stories of the Spanish Civil War (New York: Scribner's, 1969).

The Nick Adams Stories (New York: Scribner's, 1972).

The Complete Short Stories of Ernest Hemingway (New York: Scribner's, 1987).

The Collected Stories (New York: Everyman's Library, 1995).

NONFICTION WORKS

Death in the Afternoon (New York: Scribner's, 1932).

Green Hills of Africa (New York: Scribner's, 1935).

The Wild Years, ed. Gene Z. Hanrahan (New York: Dell Publishing Co., 1962).

A Moveable Feast (New York: Scribner's, 1964).

By-Line: Ernest Hemingway, ed. William White (New York: Scribner's, 1967).

Ernest Hemingway, Cub Reporter: Kansas City Star Stories, ed. Matthew J. Bruccoli (Pittsburgh, PA: University of Pittsburgh Press, 1970).

Ernest Hemingway, Selected Letters, 1917–1961, ed. Carlos Baker (New York: Scribner's, 1981).

The Dangerous Summer (New York: Scribner's, 1985).

Dateline: Toronto: The Complete Toronto Star Dispatches, 1920–1924, ed. William White (New York: Scribner's, 1985).

Ernest Hemingway on Writing, ed. Larry W. Phillips (New York: Simon and Schuster, 1999).

Hemingway on Fishing, ed. Nick Lyons (New York: Lyons Press, 2000).

Hemingway on Hunting, ed. Seán Hemingway (New York: Scribner's, 2003).

Hemingway on War, ed. Seán Hemingway (New York: Scribner's, 2003).

Under Kilimanjaro, ed. Robert W. Lewis and Robert E. Fleming (Kent, OH: Kent State University Press, 2005).

Hemingway on Paris (London: Hesperus Press, 2010).

Sites

Horton Bay General Store and Red Fox Inn

Windemere

James Beardsley Hendryx

Hearty Men and Brave Boys

December 9, 1880–March 1, 1963
Moved near Suttons Bay in 1921 and lived there the remainder of his life, writing the bulk of his fiction in a home overlooking the water

. . . .

Gold rushes are synonymous with both exalted and dashed hopes. When eighteen-year-old James Beardsley Hendryx raced to Alaska in search of fortune in 1898, he did not know that he would amass, instead of gold, other riches—material for scores of adventure stories of men at the far edge of civilization. In turn, his popularity as a writer would fulfill the young man's hopes for treasure.

Hendryx was born in Sauk Centre, Minnesota, five years earlier than fellow townsman and future Nobel Prize–winning author Sinclair Lewis. Asked in later years to compare himself to Lewis, who was known in his childhood as Red, Hendryx answered, "The difference is that Red gets a dollar a word, and I get a penny a word."[1]

Hendryx and Red's older brother, Claude, spent childhood days hunting and fishing in the woods and waters around their small hometown (and were pestered by Red for approval to join them). This passion for the outdoors would persist through life and lead to his relocation to Michigan.

Jim Hendryx left Sauk Centre while still in his adolescence to work as a cowpuncher in Montana, where he befriended two outlaws, indulging an affection for men living by their own code. In 1898, at the height of the Alaskan gold rush, Hendryx and a friend departed for Alaska and the Yukon, fueled by $1,400 in poker winnings. He spent the next fourteen months in the Yukon country, Jim said, "chopping cordwood, gouging gravel, playing poker and chopping cordwood and chopping cordwood." In other words, he did not uncover much gold.

But the author-to-be returned with other plunder. His knowledge of the gold fields and frontier translated into the narratives that would provide his living. Over the next sixty years Hendryx wrote as many as seventy novels (the exact count is imprecise) and scores of stories for pulp magazines.

Fiction writing had to wait a while. Hendryx traced his career path after his return from the gold rush: "At age 21, I was clerk in the Post Office at Sauk Centre, Minn. Also established and operated a Rural Free Delivery Route the same year. The following year I entered the U. of Minn. Law School where it took two years to prove that I would never become a great criminal lawyer."

Looking back on his academic career, Hendryx observed: "Attended public school for a vast number of years during which I learned to fish, hunt and trap ... then entered the University of Minnesota where I absorbed so much of the curriculum that even yet fragments of it work to the surface and have to be carefully removed."

After leaving the university, he said, he sold heavy hardware on the road, worked for a railway line, punched cattle for four years in Montana, was night foreman on an Ohio River dam, and sold insurance. His longest stint at a steady job was fifty-three weeks at a tannery.

Another stop on the way was journalism. Hendryx took a reporting position at the *Cincinnati Enquirer*. A legendary stunt at the *Enquirer* terminated Hendryx's career as a reporter. Hendryx covered an execution at a Joliet, Illinois, prison. It's said that he slipped a headline for the morning edition past the copyeditor: "Jenkins Jerked to Jesus at Joliet." Shortly afterward he was asked to leave. A happier Cincinnati experience was meeting and marrying Hermione Flagler, a pianist and music teacher.

Hendryx published his first novel, *The Promise: A Tale of the Great Northwest*, the tale of a dissolute young man who finds himself in the

The flamboyant James Beardsley Hendryx authored dozens of books pitting men and boys against the wilds. Courtesy of Leelanau Historical Society.

challenge of the wild, in 1915. Before long, though, he invented the characters and places that would make him famous and prosperous. Although he wrote popular Westerns, his heart was in the North.

One series born of his gold rush experience featured young Connie Morgan, a teen from the Lower forty-eight who comes to Alaska in search of his father. Learning that Sam Morgan died in a fall before he arrived, Connie chokes back tears and, in front of a group of hard-bitten but sympathetic miners, vows to remain and find the gold that eluded his father. He may be young, but the men around him recognize a stalwart spirit. "Yo'r Sam Morgan's boy all right—jest solid grit clean through. It looks f'om heah like Sam's luck has tu'ned at last!" one of them shouts.

The boy's determination sets the stage for an eventful new life. His gruff but tender friends equip him with sled dogs and guidance. Connie meets up with a new buddy, Waseche Bill, and travels to Ten Bow to join the gold rush. Bill selflessly yields his claim to Connie and departs in the night. The heart of *Connie Morgan in Alaska* is the boy's courageous search for his friend—he refuses the gift and wants to share the spoils—in the blizzards

Hendryx Park was built on a section of the property on Grand Traverse Bay that Hendryx and his wife deeded to Leelanau County. Courtesy of Joe VanderMeulen.

and vastness of the North. "Only those to whom it has been given to know the Big North—the gaunt, white, silent land beyond the haunts of men—can realize the true significance of desolation," Hendryx intones.

Connie is undaunted, dogsledding hundreds of miles solo in bitter cold and driving snow, escaping death when trapped at the end of a trail and reuniting with Waseche Bill. The duo stumbles across an Irish captive of a remote tribe, rescue him, and make a hurried, stealthy run for distant safety. After several brushes with death, the three men break through to what passes for civilization with fourteen cans of gold retrieved from a cache left by a miner who died in the wild. The miners of Ten Bow drive off Mr. Squigg, a grubby lawyer who threatens to take Connie's claim. The boy is now wealthy, and prepared for exploits detailed in later volumes, including *Connie Morgan in the Fur Country* and *Connie Morgan in the Lumber Camps*. Aimed at boys and often published first in the magazine *American Boy*, the series attracted a faithful young following.

The Halfaday Creek series won even greater rewards for Hendryx, remaining fixed enough in the minds of some that a publisher reprinted a collection of the tales in 2013. Set in the Yukon during the 1898 gold rush, more than a hundred Halfaday Creek stories were published over a quarter century for magazines such as *West*, *Dime Western*, and *New Western*.

Drawing its name from the practice of sourdoughs who pan gold half a day and play poker the other half, Halfaday Creek doesn't respect the law that applies to everyone else; it has its own code of rough justice. The town is located near the Alaska/Yukon border, providing refuge to fleeing outlaws on the run. Halfaday Creek welcomes them, protecting their anonymity and covering their tracks by requiring newcomers to choose a name from a supply on the bar. This practice avoids a surplus of John Smiths.

But tolerance ends where foul play begins. Unofficial mayor and prospector Black John keeps crime at bay in unorthodox ways. Along with Lyme "Cush" Cushing, the saloon keeper, Black John polices Halfaday Creek and deals with crime expeditiously to keep the conventional crime fighters from descending on the town and mucking up a good thing. At trial, Black John sometimes acts as both prosecutor and judge, speeding case resolution.

In "Black John Sells a Claim," Black John stands up for a young man haunted by a robbery and killing committed by his father. When the youth says he has no alternative to becoming an outlaw himself and wants a place with the gang, Black John says he does have a place. Black John then takes him out back of the saloon and points at mounds topped by wooden slabs. The boy says he doesn't understand.

"Perusal of the check letters on them slabs will help out your understandin.' M is for murdered. H is for hung. You'll note that there's quite a few more H's than M's. That's because a good many other forms of skullduggery than murder are hangable in Halfaday." The kid gets the point and stays clean.

The fictional world dreamed up by Hendryx is one in which the highest compliment is "he's a *man!*" and in which women infrequently appear. Leavened with dry humor, his novels and stories make uncomplicated and entertaining reading.

The Hendryx oeuvre won favorable reviews in respectable quarters. G. W. Harris of the *New York Times* applauded "the deftness of [plot] handling and the felicity of its writing" in *Gambler's Chance*. One entry in the Halfaday Creek series won praise from Harris as "humorous and vastly diverting." Another critic praised Hendryx's writing for its "vivid sense of place." His writing was popular enough to earn him an estimated $40,000 to $50,000 annually in the 1920s—and to be translated into Italian, German, Spanish, Portuguese, Dutch, Norwegian, and Hungarian. In 1921, a movie based on his novel *The Texan* was made. He received four other writing credits for films made between 1917 and 1923.

The author was as colorful as the characters he forged on the page. Hendryx was known as a heavy drinker, a habit picked up during his stay in the Yukon. He is supposed to have had a three-day bender with author Jack London. But he stopped drinking in 1930 after "taking the cure" at a rehabilitation center in Illinois.

Hendryx's love affair with Michigan began on a fishing trip to the Grand Traverse area hosted by author and area native Harold Titus. In 1921, Hendryx acquired three hundred acres at Lee Point near Suttons Bay and lived with his wife and their three children in, as described in a 1936 *Detroit Free Press* article, "a rambling house and log studio workshop with its oxbow over the door and a huge trap under the porch roof."

He was unapologetic about his Michigan address. "Why do I live in Northern Michigan? Well—why not?" he wrote in an autobiographical sketch.

> After knocking about through many of the states of the Union, and a good bit of Canada, I have come to the conclusion that Northern Michigan offers fewer drawbacks, and a greater number of advantages than any locality which has been my fortune, or misfortune, to have visited.
>
> Therefore, having good fishing and hunting within easy access, good schools for the children, good folks to associate with, a climate that is delightful the year round, and a firm conviction that the rest of the United States is unfit for human habitation, I live in Northern Michigan.

Hendryx liked to tap out stories in his Lee Point home on a portable typewriter perched atop a piece of hardboard in his lap. Engrossed in mental story development, he backed out of his garage once without raising the door.

On the *Information Please* radio program, host Clifton Fadiman asked the panel, "What author is noted for hunting and fishing six months of every year?"

Guest panelist Sinclair Lewis said, "James B. Hendryx."

"That's not what I have here," said Fadiman. "My script calls for Ernest Hemingway."

"That's right," Lewis admitted. "Jim Hendryx hunts and fishes twelve months of every year."

Hendryx himself turned up on a TV show. In 1956, he was fooled into traveling to Hollywood, where producers of *This Is Your Life* were waiting, along with friends. On the show, featured guests were regularly surprised to find their life stories were being told and celebrated.

A friend, Lee Smits, said, "The TV staff called me for dope on Jim. I warned them that when or where he was in the least startled, Jim would automatically let go a cuss word. Accordingly, as he was stopped on a Hollywood street and notified he was on exhibition, the TV man reached up and placed his hand before Jim's Wild Bill Hickok mustache and smothered the inevitable cuss word."

Blue language emerged on other occasions. At a family gathering in the big house on Lee Point, one of Jim's little nieces declared, "I think Uncle Jim is just like God. But I guess God probably doesn't swear as much."

Smits summed the author up: "Jim Hendryx was born 100 years too late but made the best of it. He was at heart a mountain man, a fur trader, an outlaw of the plains. He was everlastingly a boy—not a Boy Scout, more a Huckleberry Finn."

Hendryx died in 1963 after an eight-month hospital stay. He won his battle to go home to die in the company of the woods and water.

Hendryx's daughter said her father loved children and took them camping. Enjoying the same outdoors life that braced Hendryx, kids and families continue to play at Hendryx Park, a part of his property on the shores of the west arm of Grand Traverse Bay that he and his wife deeded to the public.

Works

The Promise: A Tale of the Great Northwest (New York: A.L. Burt Co., 1915).

Connie Morgan in Alaska (New York: G.P. Putnam's Sons, 1916).

The Gun-Brand (New York: A.L. Burt Co., 1917).

The Texan: A Story of the Cattle Country (New York: A.L. Burt Co., 1918).

Connie Morgan with the Mounted (New York: G.P. Putnam's Sons, 1918).

Connie Morgan in the Lumber Camps (New York: G.P. Putnam's Sons, 1919).

The Gold Girl (New York: A.L. Burt Co., 1920).

Prairie Flowers (New York: G.P. Putnam's Sons, 1920).

Connie Morgan in the Fur Country (New York: G.P. Putnam's Sons, 1921).

Snowdrift: A Story of the Land of the Strong Cold (New York: G.P. Putnam's Sons, 1922).

Connie Morgan in the Cattle Country (New York: G.P. Putnam's Sons, 1923).

North (New York: G.P. Putnam's Sons, 1923).

At the Foot of the Rainbow (New York: G.P. Putnam's Sons, 1924).

Without Gloves (New York: G.P. Putnam's Sons, 1924).

Oak and Iron (New York: G.P. Putnam's Sons, 1925).

Downey of the Mounted (New York: G.P. Putnam's Sons, 1926).

Gold and the Mounted (New York: Doubleday, Doran, 1928).

Connie Morgan Hits the Trail (New York: Doubleday, Doran, 1929).

Man of the North (Garden City, NY: Doubleday, Doran, 1929).

Blood on the Yukon Trail (New York: Doubleday, Doran, 1930).

Corporal Downey Takes the Trail (New York: Doubleday, Doran, 1931).

Grubstake Gold (New York: Doubleday, Doran, 1936).

Blood of the North (New York: Doubleday, Doran, 1938).

Hard Rock Man (New York: Carlton House [Bar H Books], 1940).

The Czar of Halfaday Creek (New York: Doubleday, Doran, 1940).

Law and Order on Halfaday Creek (New York: Carlton House, 1941).

Gold and Guns on Halfaday Creek (New York: Carlton House, 1942).

New Rivers Calling (New York: Doubleday, Doran, 1943).

Outlaws of Halfaday Creek (New York: Triangle Books, 1944).

The Saga of Halfaday Creek (Garden City, NY: Doubleday, 1947).

On the Rim of the Arctic (Garden City, NY: Doubleday, 1948).

Justice on Halfaday Creek (Garden City, NY: Doubleday, 1949).

Badmen on Halfaday Creek (Garden City, NY: Doubleday, 1950).

The Stampeders (Garden City, NY: Doubleday, 1951).

On the Rim of the Arctic (London: Museum Press Ltd., 1952).

Intrigue on Halfaday Creek (Garden City, NY: Doubleday, 1953).

Gold Is Where You Find It (New York: Doubleday [Double D Western], 1953).

Good Men and Bad (New York: Doubleday [Double D Western], 1954).

Sites

. . . .

Hendryx Park, 3705–3899 South Lee Point Road, Suttons Bay

Memorial Gardens Cemetery, 3575 Veterans Drive, Traverse City

Russell Amos Kirk

Pillar of Tradition

October 19, 1918–April 29, 1994

Born in Plymouth; graduate of and professor at Michigan State College; lived in Mecosta

· ·

The community of Plymouth in western Wayne County got its start when William Starkweather built a log cabin—actually, a shack made of young trees and bark—at the rural location now marked by a Panera Bread, a Starbucks, and a lovely shaded park that is frequently the scene of post-wedding photos and summer evening concerts. The village of Mecosta in the county of that name owes much to trees as well. Incorporated in 1883, the community enjoyed its heyday when the railroad came to town and began delivering lumber and forest products because of extensive logging of the region's old-growth forest. The railroad proved important to Plymouth also; one line cuts diagonally through the heart of town, and it meets an east-west line in picturesque Old Village. Aside from these shared Michigan attributes, both locales can boast another commonality as home to one of the greatest conservative thinkers of the contemporary era.

Russell Kirk was a prolific author with more than thirty books and hundreds of essays and reviews to his credit.[1] For three decades he edited

Russell Kirk is shown here at work in his library in the ancestral house in Mecosta. Courtesy of The Russell Kirk Center for Cultural Renewal.

the *University Bookman*, a quarterly book review, and he helped found *Modern Age*, a critical review of politics and culture. For over a decade he authored a nationally syndicated newspaper column, and for a quarter century he wrote on education for another publication that he helped launch, the *National Review*. His interests did extend beyond these achievements: he loved Gothic ghost stories and took pleasure in gardening. Tradition, though, topped everything.

Russell Kirk was born just before the Armistice ended World War I and confirmed destruction of the old order in Europe. His birth took place at home, a large Sears Roebuck bungalow near the Plymouth village railway station. His father, Russell Andrew Kirk, worked nearby at the Pere Marquette Railway yard. "Day and night, the steam locomotives puffed and hooted a few yards distant," he remembered. His mother, Marjorie Rachel Pierce, loved good poetry and inspired a love of books. Kirk recalled Plymouth as a good town to be born and grow up in, "a tranquil place" with handsome homes, tree-lined streets, and a New England–style central downtown park. His

The childhood home of Russell Kirk stood adjacent to the railway station in Plymouth.

mother's father owned F.J. Pierce's Restaurant near the tracks, a frequent stopping-in place. Another grandparent was a banker in town. Today, this part of town is known as "Old Village"; then, it housed many railroad employees.

Russell enjoyed his youth. He experienced "a cheerful infancy," though a severe illness at age three sapped his physical stamina until he reached seven. His mother's imagination and her faithfulness in reading to him, coupled with months of infirmity, drew him into the world of the intellect. He attended public school at Starkweather Elementary and the upper division at Main and Church. The Kirks were not churchgoers; Russell grew up a skeptic. He was a family man and fell under the spell of what he described as an ancestral place. It was in the "lumbering regions" of Michigan, a square-bracketed house on "Piety Hill" in Mecosta, inhabited by a great-grandmother and her two spinster daughters. He and his mother paid them frequent visits thanks to handy train connections.

Plymouth sits astride tributaries of the Rouge River; Mecosta rose up on headwaters of the Muskegon River. Lumber gave the latter town its birth and expansion, and the playing out of the forest shrank it back to hamlet size. Kirk's female relatives stayed on, barely managing to sustain a house's faded grandeur, forty acres of untillable wetlands, and some livestock. Plymouth motored on; Mecosta turned ghostly.

His education focused, he recalled with pride, on the "foundation of the book." The great classics inspired him to join the debate club and to work on the school newspaper. He claimed that he first became a writer in junior high. An essay on George Washington won a *Detroit Times* gold medal. Another on his ancestry took first place in a national competition by *Scholastic* magazine. After graduating from Plymouth High, he won a scholarship to Michigan State College. In East Lansing he received a "tolerable" liberal education, majoring in history, and he also worked on several occasions at Greenfield Village in Dearborn. Membership on the MSC debate squad took him all over the country. His team generally won. After a year obtaining a master's in history at Duke University, he came back to Michigan to work, after Pearl Harbor, in the airplane engine building at the Rouge Plant. Then he was drafted.

Kirk served four years—after induction in Detroit and training at Camp Custer—in the sparse, remote lands of Utah performing chemical warfare research. To while away the time, he wrote an article for *Michigan History* magazine about a Civil War ancestor, as well as essays for other outlets. He had no particular ambitions, and once discharged, he accepted a post at MSC and began in 1946 to teach the history of civilization. And he continued to write. With a business partner, he opened the Red Cedar Bookshop, largely stocked with secondhand books—not so much to make money as to "brew strong coffee and serve plain doughnuts and sell very good books, old and new, and have good talk." Stumbling upon a book that painted a charming picture of a Scottish university town and with nothing better in view, he decided to seek a doctor of letters in the land of his forebears. From 1948 on, he taught at Michigan State for one semester and spent the remainder of the year as a research fellow in Scotland. In 1952 he received his doctorate.

Kirk's first book was his master's thesis on the Virginia colonial figure John Randolph. The second, his doctoral dissertation at the University of St. Andrews, brought acclaim. *The Conservative Mind*, published in 1953 and made possible by a travel grant from Michigan State, was a survey of conservatism from Edmund Burke to George Santayana, covering John Adams and his son, the Virginian Randolph, James Fenimore Cooper, Nathaniel Hawthorne, and other American, British, and Irish conservatives, as well as philosophical opposites Karl Marx and John Stuart Mill. The book developed a thesis that society based on conservative principles best advances the human condition. Its surprising commercial success, both in America and Europe, enabled Kirk to eschew academia in favor of a life in letters. Much more than a polemic, the book had a literary quality that a person of any political stripe might enjoy:

> Walk beside the Liffey in Dublin, a little way west of the dome of the Four Courts, and you come to an old doorway in a blank wall. This is the roofless wreck of an eighteenth-century house, and until recently the house still was here, inhabited although condemned. Number 12, Arran Quay, formerly a brick building of three stories, which began as a gentleman's residence, sank to the condition of a shop, presently was used as a government office of the meaner sort, and was demolished in 1950—a history suggestive of changes on a mightier scale since 1729, in Irish society. For in that year, Edmund Burke, the greatest native of Ireland, was born here . . . And you may reflect, with Burke, "What shadows we are, and what shadows we pursue!"

Kirk was thirty-five years old when his magnum opus made its first splash. Over his lifetime it sold one million copies in seven editions, thanks in large part, he asserted, to its engaging style.

In his memoirs, written in the third person, Kirk summarized who he was:

> His was no Enlightenment mind . . . it was a Gothic mind, medieval in its temper and structure. He did not love cold harmony and perfect regularity of organization; what he sought was a complex of variety, mystery, tradition, the venerable, the awful.

It was a mind that railed against those who would impose on the world "a dreary conformity." He had an antipathy to efficiency and progress; he embraced diversity and tradition. He felt that the "unreasoning forces of industrialism, centralization, secularism, and the leveling impulse" must be opposed. Reviews upon the issuance of *The Conservative Mind*—even in the liberal *New York Times*—were highly complimentary. It remains "conservatism's most highly regarded resource for heritage and scholarly authority."[2]

Kirk defined conservatism as "preservation of the ancient moral traditions of humanity." He framed it in six essential principles or "canons," which he would amend from time to time, just as he would tinker with the lineup of the conservative thinkers discussed in succeeding versions. First was belief that a divine intent rules society and conscience; second was affection for the ever-increasing variety and mystery of life; third, civil society requires order and classes, and the only true equality is moral equality; fourth, property and freedom are inextricably connected; fifth, law and tradition provide checks upon humanity's will and appetite; and sixth, change and reform are not identical; slow change is preferable to radicalism.

Also constant were his convictions about the evils of centralized political power, egalitarian economic policies, oppressive bureaucracy, and fiscal imprudence. Disclaiming hubris, he thought the book essential, for the world needed conservative renewal after two world wars, violent revolutions, and uncontrolled change had torn global society apart. He advocated a return to "the reign of law, the traditions of civility, the sense of community, and the family." He lamented the homogenization of the university—and notably, Michigan State. Rather than its rapid and extensive expansion under President John Hannah, Kirk preferred the school to remain modestly sized and emphasize quality over breadth, tradition over innovation.

Kirk saw the American Revolution as a conservative rebellion against the departure from tradition imposed by the Crown. Lest anyone think he justified human bondage as a legitimate societal foundation, Kirk termed it a detestable and great evil. Yet he lamented what the "Civil War and the suppression of the South" had done: slavery should not be remedied by "legislative contrivance," but by other, more peaceable means. Kirk protested how the state, not the individual, had become the "main organ of authority in society." He felt that once culture in America had become "wholly subordinated to economic appetite" through urbanization, the automobile, and government expansion, the nation had lost its soul. Still, he believed that democracy would endure.

The man from strait-laced Plymouth was no stern moralist. He enjoyed irony, and his favorite definition of "conservative" was that of satirist Ambrose

Bierce: "a statesman who is enamored of existing evils, as distinguished from the Liberal who wishes to replace them with others." The twists and turns in his life amused him, for he had never imagined becoming an internationally known author.

On September 19, 1964, another twist occurred when he married Annette Courtemanche, whom he met due to a speaking engagement that she attended as president of the student body at Molloy College on Long Island. She was twenty years his junior; it was a marriage of like minds. They honeymooned on Beaver Island in Lake Michigan, where his wife noticed his preference for writing rather than talking. She did not mind. She reported that one of the few subjects about which they did not see eye to eye was the way from Grand Rapids to Mecosta after a trip out of state: "whether we should drive home the 70 miles from the airport via the expressway or the scenic route. I'll leave it to you to guess who always wanted to take the scenic route."

Kirk embraced the "Gothick" not just theoretically but in ghost stories he wrote. *Ancestral Shadows* is a collection of nineteen of his best, including stories about "haunted St. Andrews" and his "own ancestral spooky house." The book jacket of *Old House of Fear* described the author as "quite at home among ghosts. He lives alone in an old frame house on the eerie pine barrens of Mecosta." Another went further to picture him "writing from his haunted house at Mecosta, one of the most isolated places on earth." An anomaly, these flights of imagination? Not in Kirk's eyes, for his autobiography recounts several unaccountable visions experienced by family members and his own. He maintained that worthwhile literature always "has some ethical end." He fashioned these ghost stories as morality fables juxtaposing evil and good and, rather than frivolous, he felt they "can be an instrument for the recovery of moral order." In several, government employees—such as a planning officer and a census taker—confront powers far beyond their own.

Putting the scare into government minions formed the purpose of several of his opinion pieces. In his 1968 article "Politician, Spare that Dome," Kirk denigrated the "crew of barbarous innovators" who sought to erect a new capitol in Lansing. The "vandals" advocated that "anything 'modern' must be better than anything venerable," but historic buildings remind us "that we are heirs to an ancient patrimony, and that we have duties toward those yet unborn." He quoted Edmund Burke's sage observation that love of country requires that "our country ought to be lovely."

A year later, "Pulling Down Everything Interesting" decried how the typical American city was becoming dull, dreary, and featureless thanks to a mania of demolishing historical structures. Kirk's specific focus was saving the clock tower of the Grand Rapids City Hall, since the building's destruction was ordained. The tower was "a romantic Gothic structure," and its preservation would prove foresighted: "Those cities that act today to save something of their architectural patrimony will be envied by other cities within a few years." City fathers saved only a couple things; the original clock faces and entrance coping remain in testimony to a lack of vision near the steps to the blandly modern county courthouse. Kirk's To the Point column proved prescient.

Sticking to his principles, Kirk did not favor the presidential candidacies of moderates Dwight Eisenhower or Gerald Ford. His hopes were pinned on conservatives Robert Taft, Barry Goldwater, and Ronald Reagan. Regardless of who held office or sought it, Kirk did not want and refused to accept appointments. Just as he felt he had more utility as a writer than as a professor, Kirk chose the path less traveled when it came to political office. His writing served in the stead of exercising power. In 1989, he received the Presidential Citizens Medal for "exemplary deeds of service" to country and fellow citizens.

After his bestseller enabled self-described retirement to Mecosta and Piety Hill, Kirk upheld tradition and invested in the family property. He acquired an adjacent barn for his trove of books and purchased a house there for his father and stepmother. He composed on a typewriter on the top floor until fire destroyed the ancient clapboard house in 1975. Disdaining to move elsewhere, he replaced it with a brick Italianate structure. From these family quarters—frequently opened to students in seminars and informal gatherings—he continued to write books, columns, and articles. For thirty-three years, the *University Bookman* issued from Mecosta. As did his ancestor, he went to battle on behalf of the causes he believed in, an indefatigable author at his duty station in the cutover lands.

A daughter would recount that when her father moved to Piety Hill, the land had been "shaved of its lush trees by the family's first settlers, earning it the name 'Stump Country.'" Kirk embraced that past. He took pride in being a "stump dodger"—in the "old-fangled village" where his family had roots, where "on a glaciated slope above a creek that flows into the Little Muskegon" was found continuity while America proceeded to throw out the old in favor of the new. Mecosta was where "the country spirit is alive and well" and where, to conservationists' delight, he planted thousands of trees on the property and its environs. Here was pure air, spaciousness, quietude. Old woodland trails, an abundance of lakes, boulder-strewn streams—he wrote of these natural charms in a travel article, praising the small establishments in the region run and patronized by big-hearted people. His daughter also said, "the most precious objects in my father's life were his family, his home, and his five acres of land."

Besides reaping all the sales, he received a dozen honorary doctorates and an award for his fiction. Still, his situation merited an assessment in a 1984 *Wall Street Journal* column that "his work has received little attention from the intellectual establishment." It put the blame squarely on his decision to live and work where his ancestors had founded a lumber town rather than in the intellectual centers of New York and Washington.

Kirk died on April 28, 1994. Burial was in Saint Michaels Cemetery outside of Remus on the road from Mecosta toward M-66. His gravestone replicates the type found in old Scottish churchyards, bearing a Celtic inscription along with "Man of Letters" and a quote from T. S. Eliot: "The communication of the dead is tongued with fire beyond the language of the living."

Plymouth no longer is home to the Daisy air rifle plant that Kirk knew as a youngster; the only traces are a sign and a condominium project bearing the name. The pioneer Wilcox mill he once wrote about in a short story was replaced by a Ford Motor cottage-industry plant that became part of the Arsenal of Democracy, now itself the victim of neglect. The municipality still hails itself as the City of Homes. The town remains a rail crossroads, and Old Village still retains many of the buildings that Kirk knew. Passenger service is gone, but the memories of great trains of America still echo across the landscape and hurtle on, Wolfeian, toward their destinations over the everlasting earth. The Plymouth train station also stands, a monument to how Kirk came and went, and ultimately left for fortune, fame, and happiness in, of all places, the stumpland.

Piety Hill, the Kirk house, remains on the southwest corner of the intersection of M-20 and Franklin Street in Mecosta. The Russell Kirk Center for Cultural Renewal is a block away in a building on Franklin Street between Moore and Maple. Kirk's legacy continues in a town taking its name from a Potawatomi chief. For a mind that was centered on "first principles," the continuity seems, well, purely Michigan.

Works

Randolph of Roanoke: A Study in Conservative Thought (Chicago: University of Chicago, 1951).

The Conservative Mind: From Burke to Santayana (Chicago: H. Regnery Co., 1953).

St. Andrews (London: B.T. Batsford Ltd., 1954).

A Program for Conservatives (Chicago: H. Regnery Co., 1954).

Academic Freedom: An Essay in Definition (Chicago: H. Regnery Co., 1955).

Beyond the Dreams of Avarice: Essays of a Social Critic (Chicago: H. Regnery Co., 1956).

The American Cause (Chicago: H. Regnery Co., 1957).

The Intelligent Woman's Guide to Conservatism (New York: Devin-Adair Co., 1957).

Old House of Fear (New York: Fleet Publishing Corp., 1961).

The Surly Sullen Bell: Ten Stories and Sketches, Uncanny or Uncomfortable, with a Note on the Ghostly Tale (New York: Fleet Publishing Corp., 1962).

Confessions of a Bohemian Tory: Episodes and Reflections of a Vagrant Career (New York: Fleet Press Corp., 1963).

The Intemperate Professor, and Other Cultural Splenetics (Baton Rouge: Louisiana State University Press, 1965).

A Creature of the Twilight: His Memorials (New York: Fleet Publishing Corp., 1966).

Edmund Burke: A Genius Reconsidered (New Rochelle, NY: Arlington House, 1967).

The Political Principles of Robert A. Taft (with James McClellan) (New York: Fleet Press Corp., 1967).

Enemies of the Permanent Things: Observations of Abnormity in Literature and Politics (New Rochelle, NY: Arlington House, 1969).

Eliot and His Age: T. S. Eliot's Moral Imagination in the Twentieth Century (New York: Random House, 1971).

The Roots of American Order (La Salle, IL: Open Court, 1974).

Decadence and Renewal in the Higher Learning: An Episodic History of American University and College since 1953 (South Bend, IN: Gateway Editions, 1978).

John Randolph of Roanoke: A Study in American Politics, with Selected Speeches and Letters (Indianapolis: Liberty Press, 1978).

Lord of the Hollow Dark (New York: St. Martin's Press, 1979).

The Princess of All Lands (Sauk City, WI: Arkham House Publishers, 1979).

The Portable Conservative Reader (Chicago: Penguin Books, 1982).

Watchers at the Strait Gate (Sauk City, WI: Arkham House Publishers, 1984).

The Wise Men Know What Wicked Things Are Written on the Sky (Washington, DC: Regnery Gateway, 1987).

Economics: Work and Prosperity (Pensacola, FL: Beka Book, 1988).

America's British Culture (New Brunswick, NJ: Transaction Publishers, 1993).

The Politics of Prudence (Bryn Mawr, PA: Intercollegiate Studies Institute, 1993).

The Sword of Imagination: Memoirs of a Half-Century of Literary Conflict (Grand Rapids, MI: Eerdmans Publishing Co., 1995).

Redeeming the Time (with Jeffrey O. Nelson) (Wilmington, DE: Intercollegiate Studies Institute, 1996). *Rights and Duties: Reflections on Our Conservative Constitution* (with Mitchell S. Muncy) (Dallas: Spence Publishing Co., 1997). *Ancestral Shadows: An Anthology of Ghostly Tales* (with Vigen Guroian) (Grand Rapids, MI: Eerdmans Publishing Co., 2004).

Sites

Plymouth home, 873 N. Mill Street
Kirk House, Mecosta
Kirk Library, Mecosta
Grave in Saint Michaels Cemetery, M-20 at 50th Avenue, Remus, Mecosta County

Della Thompson Lutes

Gallant Figure

September 1867–July 13, 1942

Born in Jackson County; graduate of Jackson High School; taught grade school in Jackson, Hanover, Horton, Grass Lake, Detroit

. . . .

This is the Hour of Lead.—EMILY DICKINSON, "After Great Pain, a Formal Feeling Comes"

Jackson, Michigan, has been called "Jacktown" for a long time, thanks to a state maximum-security prison that in the mid-twentieth century brought fame to the mid-Michigan city. The "Big House" obscured the town's origin and heritage, its naming after the first Democratic Party president, and its distinction as birthplace of the Republican Party. The county of the same name is host to some of the best parks in the state. Communities named Pulaski, Waterloo, Hanover, and Napoleon confirm that early on it was the refuge of European immigrants seeking opportunity without forgetting their former homes.

In July 2014, Jackson drew notice because of the descendant of an émigré, a woman named Paula Faris, born and raised there. The granddaughter of Lebanese immigrants, she had been promoted to anchor for ABC's *Good Morning America Weekend*. The spotlight brought her into the ranks of other Jacksonians like footballer Tony Dungy, astronaut James McDivitt, entertainer Jack Paar, and Supreme Court justice Potter Stewart. Down in a corner of the county, Brooklyn's Michigan International Speedway is one of motorsports' premier facilities.

Locally born Della Thompson rarely makes lists. She is not of the vintage of the Paars and Stewarts, having lived and died seven decades ago. Her childhood unfolded during a much slower era. For over seventy years, though, her life was as full of travails and triumphs as any of these notables.

She was born in September 1867—she always kept the actual date to herself—the only child of pioneers Elijah Bonnett Thompson and Almira Frances Bogardus. In the 1870s their home was on a farm in Summit Township where Marion Road dead-ends at Hague Road, near today's village of Vandercook Lake. Farm life was rich in family but not financially. When she was twelve, her aged father (twenty years older than "Delly's" mother) sold the farm and moved them into the southern part of the town of Jackson, near the Griswold Park school. He traded farming for carpentry. She "exchanged a country school for a graded one."

Della graduated at age sixteen from Jackson High School, bright and motivated, then qualified by examination to teach in the district schools. Despite her youth, she found jobs in the communities of South Jackson, Horton, Hanover, and Grass Lake over the next three years. At age nineteen she accepted a teaching position in Detroit, where she taught for a time at the Grove School until marriage in 1893 to Louis Irving Lutes, a bicycle dealer in the city. They had two sons: Ralph Irving, born in May 1894, and Robert Brosseau Lutes, born in December 1897. She had home economics skills as well. The Lutes' home at 423 Baldwin became a center for neighborhood life. Mrs. Lutes was credited with organizing the "Detroit Homemakers" women's club and remained a lifelong honorary member. She also became a member of a similar organization, the Women Writers Club of Detroit.[1]

The WWCD had been known first as the Detroit Women's Press Club. Mrs. Lutes qualified for membership because she had been published, attributing her initial compensated work to a piece in the *Detroit Free Press*. By January 1906, author Della Thompson Lutes was publishing a five-part story entitled "Deestrick No. 5" in the periodical *Delineator*, had written for the *Detroit*

Della Thompson Lutes poses with a domestic felicity that conceals her life's heartaches. Courtesy of the Clarke Historical Library, Central Michigan University.

News-Tribune and numerous periodicals such as *Good Housekeeping* and children's and mothers' magazines, and served as editor for *Youth's Outlook*. She accomplished this work despite the burden of other responsibilities: "the care of two little boys and an aged mother has left her little time for writing."[2]

Care was transformed into grief when Ralph died in an accident. His bereaved mother dealt with her loss through art, and in 1906 appeared the novel *Just Away: A Story of Hope*. The book derived its title from a poem by James Whitcomb Riley in which a young man's premature death is lamented: "I can not say, and I will NOT say / That he is dead. He is just away." The dedication, written in Detroit on February 12, 1906, was "to the mothers who sorrowed with me in my sorrow; the mothers with whom I have grieved in their grief; and the great host of stricken hearts the world over who are mourning." Rather than autobiography, Lutes employed fiction to deal with her loss in order to grapple with "the mystery that has for ages racked men's souls."

In *Just Away*, childless Jean resides in the home of her lifelong friend Helen, a teacher and wife to Maurice. Their seven-year-old son[3] Berger, brother to younger Lysbeth, has recently died. Jean is no stranger to loss, for "one by one" her loved ones have perished. The boy was Jean's "name-child," and she suffers

Lutes's early years were spent in this gentle country setting, south of Jackson.

his loss as much as his parents do. Helen's grief is her "first great sorrow." Her mother had been taciturn and puritanical, her father improvident and agnostic. The four survivors try to live on in Helen's childhood home in their little village. When despair threatens to consume the grieving mother, she seeks counsel from the local minister. He advises that she "must just simply trust." For one without spiritual foundations, the message seems unhelpful, even hurtful, and Helen spirals into hopelessness, feeling as "if things were slipping, slipping away." Desperation draws her onto her knees one evening, Scriptures open before her. A ray of light appears, followed by days and nights of meditation, contemplative conversations with Jean as they sit before the parlor window, and visits by encouraging friends and neighbors.

Over time, Helen comes to a place in her heart where she finds hope for—and has confidence in—Berger's well-being in a joy-filled life hereafter. Then, a letter arrives from Helen's sister-in-law Kate, advising that she will pay a very short visit. "Her youngest child, a little girl of four had but recently died, and the mother could not endure the loneliness of her home, and was going for a long visit to relatives in California, hoping to forget her agony of grief in change of scene." Maurice's family had disapproved of his marriage to Helen, believing she was beneath him. Kate's stay, though brief, could continue that coldness. Still, feeling a kindred tie through loss, Helen welcomes the visit.

The remainder of the story centers on how Kate, at first disapproving of Helen and bitter over her own fate, comes to appreciate the once-hidden grace that has saved her brother's wife. Initially Helen's message is one of patience: "I don't mean that you will ever lose the grief . . . but I mean that you will learn how to bear it." Through their time together, Kate softens, puts aside her adherence to traditional mourning, and seeks insight from the working girl she had formerly disdained. On an April evening that "had grown cool, and rain was threatening, and the fire sent a glow and warmth through the rooms that was very grateful," the three women sit down to contend with Kate's sobs and her challenge: "I cannot feel resignation over the loss of my child." Helen's gentle response is "*Have* you lost her, sister Kate?" "I can't do for her, or love her," comes the reply. "Oh, my dear, my dear," Helen quickly answers, with the central message of *Just Away*:

> Don't say that. And she isn't put beyond your reach forever; only for a few, few years. At the most, but a little while, and in the meantime you can love her . . . and do for her. You cannot help loving her. All the love she brought with her when she came to you; all that grew with her, as she grew, is in your heart and will remain there until you meet. You must go on loving her more and more every day until you hold her in your arms again.

Helen is no blind believer; she admits to "seasons of doubt." But an unshakable faith in the future helps her persevere and comfort an in-law who becomes a sister, sharing a bond the women had never held or sought. A changed Kate decides not to continue seeking escape, for there are "so many hearts to comfort. So many fallen ones to raise. So many cheering words to be spoken . . . There may be those at home who are mourning, too, and they cannot run away. I shall go home, and we will bear it together." As the book closes, the two friends visit Berger's grave in the cemetery "which had held so much of awe for us as children, and now contained so large a part of our lives that it seemed quite like going home."

Though not specifically set in Michigan, the work is clearly autobiographical. The pastoral environs—village, woods and flowers, moss and meadows, streams and rivers, and a beautiful house "overhung with fragrant, flowering vines, set in a garden of sweetest blossoms"—draw on Lutes's memories of growing up in Jackson. The book might not be suitable for those in the immediate throes of loss, but it was not meant for all audiences.

Later, Lutes would write of these awful days in first person. Of how "when a little boy went suddenly away, I could not endure the sight of all the things his warm small hands had suddenly dropped. Fear was with me then. Fear that he *was not*, or fear that he *was*, and crying for me in his fright and loneliness." Coming to believe in a "kindly Father to whom I might intrust [*sic*] him," she decided her little boy was safe and, "knowing then . . . I brought out his drum again and hung it over my desk, so as to keep him near me."

When the United States entered World War I, another challenge loomed. Remaining son Robert enlisted. As she had after the loss of her first boy, Lutes took to writing. *My Boy in Khaki: A Mother's Story* begins poignantly: "I can hear nothing but the shriek of the train that bore him away and the grind of the wheels as the crowd bent back to let them turn . . . Sore as our hearts were, and blurred though the proudly marching line was to our eyes, we thrilled, and waved our flags, and cheered—when we did not choke." She wondered if the war would mean a return visit by the "Great Gray Wolf of Tragedy." It was in "writing of the present pain, I find relief in tears, and, soothed, go about my work again." Like many military mothers throughout the ages, she supported her son in his decision, reluctantly let him go, and struggled to find confidence in his well-being. To her great relief, Robert returned safely from overseas.

These two works predate the homey autobiographical style for which Lutes would later gain wide readership. Centered on cooking and the country kitchen, her later books wove a nostalgia that won her acclaim. Critics rarely if ever noted the hard foundation in the difficult early books that they followed.

The first was published by a firm in Cooperstown, New York. The village was home to *American Motherhood*, and in 1907 the Lutes moved there so that Della could take a position on the editorial staff of the Curtis publication. Five years later she became editor in chief. Over time she served as editor of *Table Talk* and *Today's Housewife*. She also wrote for other periodicals, including *American Mercury, Century Magazine, Forum, Saturday Review of Literature*, and the *Atlantic*.

Not long after the family relocated to New York, the marriage foundered. In the 1918 *My Boy in Khaki* she wrote of having no parents, no living relative other than distant cousins, and no husband. In the 1920 census, she is listed as the "head" of the household at 14 Chestnut in Cooperstown, with the only other occupant a "lodger." Lutes's occupation is "editor" for a "publ. co."—and with this notation: "D" for divorced. Robert, employed as "art editor" for a "publ. house," lived on 38 Elm Street with his wife Cecily. Louis I. Lutes, by contrast, lived in Oneida with his current wife Harriette. In little more than a decade, domestic harmony had ended.

In 1923, Lutes moved to Boston to edit *Modern Priscilla*. One of her tasks was to oversee the "proving plant" for the publication, today referred to as a test kitchen. She also hosted a radio show every Tuesday and Thursday on WNAC-Boston. The passage of time—she was now in her late fifties—had brought on physical ailments. Suffering from crippling arthritis and worsening eyesight, she spoke in 1937 of how mere walking was extremely painful. Still, "she never stopped working."

Domestic affairs were her signature. *The Country Kitchen* reached back to the nineteenth century and to her childhood home. The American Booksellers Association voted it an award as "The Most Original Book Published in 1936." It became a bestseller, reprinted eight times in the next five months, fifteen over the following five years, and again in 1992 by Wayne State University. It contained reminiscences besides recipes: "The very walls of the kitchen were permeated with the odors of roast meat, salt-rising bread, spice cake, gingerbread—a whole roster of fragrant memories, tantalizing to the nose and stimulating to the palate." *Time* highlighted her on December 12, 1938, under the heading "Nostalgia." Occurring when she was nearly seventy, the book's success encouraged her to write several more in the same vein over the next six years, and the public bought them up. Each made food a central feature, "the embodiment of life at its most complete and satisfying."[4] The place where it was prepared, the setting for the lives remembered, was equally so.

On July 13, 1942, Lutes died suddenly of a heart attack. Her ashes were brought back to Jackson County, to a little country cemetery south of Horton, to the plot of a friend with whom she had often stayed during visits

The simple gravestone of Della Thompson Lutes plainly evidences her vocation.

to Michigan. Among the tributes were these: she was "a woman of tolerance, understanding, and broad sympathies," "the salt of the earth, and it's the earth that has lost some of its savor with her going." An open book marks the headstone.

One friendly critic contends "that her writings are unusual and that their uniqueness urges that they deserve to be more widely known than they are."[5] Her books debuted "during a period when the swiftly-growing numbers of newly urbanized Americans were discovering the nostalgic appeal of their own recent background."[6] University of Michigan English scholar Carlton F. Wells went so far as to call *The Country Kitchen* an American classic. No less an authority than Bruce Catton relied on it in his bicentennial history of the state. Terming it a delightful book on Michigan, he included it on a list of suggested readings. Catton quoted the pioneer's daughter in a passage describing how life was once idyllic in Michigan, full of peace, plenty, and simple happiness.

In an account of a visit to Jackson not long before her death, Lutes spoke of "the Grand River puddling along," of "the tamarack swamp where I used to go to find tamarack gum, and a little of the osage-orange my father planted."

Despite life's disappointments, she continued to extol her Michigan youth, as in the final words of her classic, recounting the time after the Christmas meal was over, guests had left, and family remained:

The day was drawing to its early close. The skies were lowering, gray and threatening. It would snow before night set in. My father went to the front room to nod and doze. My mother and Miz' Esty returned to the kitchen and lighted the lamps. The work was not quite finished. Miz' Esty, with a full-gathered gingham apron tied over an equally full-gathered and many-gored woolen skirt, washed the dishes while my mother dried and put them away. The room smelled pleasantly of food mingled with the odor of geranium leaves and damp earth. My mother had been pouring tea on her plants. A cat crouched over a plate near the door. Another cat could be seen stretched at length upon my father's knee. The dog, Shep, lay just outside upon the step, hopefully waiting for snow.

The women talked softly together. Their voices drifted in and out of the warmth of the room, the shadows from the lamp, the homely fragrance. The fire burned low in the stove. My mother opened the lid and thrust in a couple of sticks. It would be allowed, later, to go out for the night. We would eat bread and milk for supper.

It had been a good day, after all. Nothing to make history, but good to live, good to remember . . .

[Rousing himself, her father asks for her help in the barn.] The light from the kitchen streams out—a lovely light—soft, lambent, and golden like a heavenly road to peace and safety. Here in the barn there is security. Storms cannot enter. Nothing can harm us here, for my father is in charge. The animals trust him. I trust him.

Back there in the kitchen is safety, too. Warmth, and light, and food—and Mother.

Works

. . . .

Just Away: A Story of Hope (Cooperstown, NY: Crist, Scott & Parshall, 1906).
The Beginning of Life (Philadelphia: After School Club of America, 1911).
Bible Stories from the Old Testament: Retold for Children (Cooperstown, NY: Arthur H. Crist Co., 1911).

Child, Home and School: Mothers' and Teachers' Club Booklet (with Elizabeth Evans
  Pettinger) (Cooperstown, NY: Arthur H. Crist Co., 1911).

The Secrets of Life (New York: N.p., circa 1911).

The Story of Life for Children (Cooperstown, NY: Arthur H. Crist Co., 1914).

My Boy in Khaki: A Mother's Story (New York: Harper and Brothers, 1918).

The Gracious Hostess: A Book of Etiquette (Indianapolis: Bobbs-Merrill Co., 1923).

*Modern Priscilla Cook Book: One Thousand Recipes Tested and Proved at the
  Priscilla Proving Plant* (Boston: Priscilla Publishing Co., 1924).

*Modern Priscilla Home Furnishing Book: A Practical Book for the Woman Who
  Loves Her Home* (Boston: Priscilla Publishing Co., 1925).

A Home of Your Own (Indianapolis: Bobbs-Merrill Co., 1925).

Table Setting and Service for Mistress and Maid (Boston: M. Barrows & Co., 1928).

Bridge Food for Bridge Fans (Boston: M. Barrows & Co., 1932).

A Book of Menus with Recipes (New York: G.P. Putnam's Sons, 1936).

The Country Kitchen (Boston: Little, Brown and Co., 1936).

Home Grown (Boston: Little, Brown and Co., 1937).

Millbrook (Boston: Little, Brown and Co., 1938).

Gabriel's Search (Boston: Little, Brown and Co., 1940).

Country Schoolma'am (Boston: Little, Brown and Co., 1941).

Cousin William (Boston: Little, Brown and Co., 1942).

Sites

Home site, Floyd Avenue at Hague Avenue, Vandercook Lake, Summit Township,
  Jackson County

Home site, Griswold Street at Kibby Road, City of Jackson

Infants School site, Hanover Road at Thorne, Liberty Township, Jackson County

Grove Elementary School (now Cornerstone–Grove School), 13436 Grove Street,
  Detroit

423 Baldwin, Detroit

Horton Cemetery, west of the Moscow Road/Tripp Road intersection, Horton,
  Jackson County, Section 3, Lot 248

Exhibit, Michigan Historical Museum, Lansing

Moore and Guest

Hometown Poets

Julia Ann Moore (December 1, 1847–June 5, 1920)
Born in Plainfield; lived in Edgerton and Manton

Edgar Albert Guest (August 20, 1881–August 5, 1959)
Lived, went to school, and worked in Detroit[1]

. . . .

Literary is a work very difficult to do.—JULIA ANN MOORE

In December 1997, the governor of Michigan issued a proclamation enjoining all citizens to celebrate the "many contributions to our unique American culture" of the "Sweet Singer of Michigan." Every Michigander was to observe how "the Great Lakes State is truly fortunate to include a person of Julia A. Moore's talent and character as part of its historic past." Born on December 1, 1847, in Plainfield Township, Julia Ann Davis had overcome many hurdles for her poetry to be so recognized.

Half a century earlier on March 1952, the Michigan legislature adopted a resolution proclaiming Edgar A. Guest the "Poet Laureate of the state of Michigan." It was formal recognition that "people of the State of Michigan throughout the years have looked to the poems of Edgar A. Guest for moral support in times of stress and have enjoyed his subtle humor and sound homespun philosophy."[2] The people were to rely on Michigan's poet laureate for encouragement during hard times to come, as they always do in the Mitten State. A poem can act "as a doorway that connects the room of the invisible with the room of the visible."[3]

When Moore's poems first appeared in 1876, the nation had just emerged from the most traumatic and bloody conflict in its history; U.S. troops continued to enforce federal law in the South, the race issue had made little progress, and an economic slump troubled the country's centennial. Between October 1873 and March 1879, the U.S. economy shrank by two-thirds. The sixty-five-month downturn remains the longest and deepest plunge in American history, surpassing both the Great Depression of the 1930s and the recession of the 2000s. People needed a diversion to boost spirits and inspire hope. Moore helped serve that purpose.

Julia Davis was the eldest child in an impoverished Kent County family. Limited to a few years of schooling—of uncertain quality—she became a homemaker at age ten when her mother's severe illness required her to take on adult duties. Once in her teens, she found time to write verse for her own entertainment. A later poem about this stage paints a picture much brighter than one might imagine, beginning with the memory that "my childhood days were happy":

I am not ashamed of my birthright,
Though it was of poor estate,
Many a poor person in our land
Has risen to be great.

My parents were poor, I know, kind friends,
But that is no disgrace;
They were humble and respected
Throughout my native place.

My mother was an invalid,
And was for many a year,
And I being the eldest daughter
Her life I had to cheer.

I had two little sisters,
And a brother which made three,
And dear mother being sickly,
Their care fell on me.

She also possessed an ambition perhaps surprising for such humble circumstances:

My heart was gay and happy,
This was ever in my mind,
There is better times a coming,
And I hope some day to find
Myself capable of composing.
It was my heart's delight,
To compose on a sentimental subject
If it came in my mind just right.

Repetitiveness and inapt verbs reveal the author's inadequate education. The gist, though, demonstrates an admirable strength of character.

At age seventeen she married and moved to a farm one mile west of Edgerton, just north of Rockford. Husband Frederick Moore tolerated her creativity so long as she fulfilled duty to home and hearth. Theirs was no one-way relationship, as she would later record:

Dearest love, do you remember,
The first time that we met—
Our youthful days have gone, love,
I hope you love me yet,
Now we are growing old, love,
Our heads will soon be gray,
May we ever love each other
Till from earth we pass away.

In a similar sentimental remembrance, she talked of the relationship with her parents:

Oh! my mother, how I love her,
Though her head is growing gray,

For in fancy I can see her
Bending o'er me night and day,

. . . .

Oh! my father, how I love him,
For he has worked hard for me,
For to earn my food and clothing,
In my little infancy.
And oh, I will not forget him,
While on earth I do remain—
May the God of heaven bless him
In this world of grief and pain.[4]

In 1876 Grand Rapids publisher C. M. Loomis issued a compilation of
Moore's poems under the title *The Sentimental Song Book*. It was the centennial year; thus the contents dealt with the national commemoration and
other popular topics, many of which "were intended to be sung to contemporary melodies."[5] A year later, Cleveland publisher James F. Ryder reissued
the volume of poetry and, apparently, first applied to her the honorific of
"The Sweet Singer of Michigan." Honor may not have been his goal; in a letter transmitting the book to reviewers and outlets he offered this assessment:

> Dear Sir—Having been honored by the gifted lady of Michigan, in being entrusted
> with the publication of her poems, I give myself the pleasure of handing you a
> copy of the same, with my respectful compliments.
>
> It will prove a health lift to the overtaxed brain; it may divert the despondent
> from suicide. It should enable the reader to forget the "stringency," and guide the
> thoughts into pleasanter channels . . . It must be productive of good to humanity.
>
> If you have the good of your fellow creatures at heart, and would contribute
> your mite towards putting them in the way to finding this little volume, the thanks
> of a grateful people (including authoress and publisher) would be yours.
>
> If a sufficient success should attend the sale of this work, it would be our pur-
> pose to complete the Washington monument.

The obelisk commemorating the Father of His Country would not be
completed until 1884. One entry, entitled "Beautiful Twenty-Second," did
hail the day in February, "we love it dear," on which "Columbia's noblest son"

Edgar A. Guest celebrated with friends on his seventy-fourth birthday, which marked the beginning of his seventh decade in newspapering. Tony Spina Collection, Walter P. Reuther Library, Archives of Labor and Urban Affairs, Wayne State University.

was born. Finishing the National Mall monument from the sale of this slim poetry collection seems a jest.

Reviews started pouring in that excoriated and ridiculed the poetess's style and subjects. True, many entries began with the exhortation "Come, my friends," or similar variations. True, many dealt with "morbid" subjects such as accidental death and the loss of children to disease. One poem entitled "Ashtabula Disaster" recalled the collapse of a railroad bridge under the weight of a train, resulting in numerous fatalities. True, her live public readings could amuse audiences to the point of boisterous jibing. Her protective husband forbade the publication—not necessarily the creation—of more poetry after a second volume failed and ticketholders could not be trusted to behave during her performances.[6] That book mustered only seven new poems; the first eighty pages were devoted to friendly reviews in a valiant attempt to defend the author. Thereafter, Moore would write for friends, not for broad publication.

The horse-drawn cart frequented for late-night meals by a youthful Guest and Henry Ford
is known now as the "Owl Night Lunch" wagon.

Perhaps in order to protect her, or simply to find a better farm, Mr. Moore moved the family (Julia bore him ten children, of whom six survived) a hundred miles north to the town of Manton in Wexford County in 1882. Here, perhaps, they could escape notoriety. They could not avoid interest. A year later, a student journal at the University of Michigan solicited a new effort. Presuming that the *Argonaut* would publish her entry unvarnished, as it claimed, she failed to obscure the lack of schooling arising from the loss of her mother:

> sir. your favor of the 1th is at hand in reply would say I havent wrote any for nearly
> 2 years . . . I did intend never to write any more; at Mr. Moore request I answer yu
> letter. He says I would send one verse and chorus and see what they will do with
> it. you see I have been abused by the press, I know not my friends.

Accompanying were the sought-after single verse and chorus of "The Young Student," to wit:

Yonder stands a noble scholar on the hill;

Looking back o'er his pathway with joy.

He is thinking how with energy and will,

He has risen to the top; while yet a boy.

Even now he is thinking of the past.

How the future to him, once, look'd dim,

How by working he has climb the hill; at last,

There's a light in the future for him.

Chorus

There's a light, in the future,

There's a light, in the future,

There's a light in the future, for him.

If he works with all his might;

With God, upon the right;

There's a light, in the future, for him.

The student editor was bemused: "It would be a labor of love to point out the beauties of this choice fragment, its adorable simplicity, its novel punctuation, its jaunty metre; but why gild pure gold? Why paint the lily? Give thee good den, sweet Julia."[7]

Her pen fell silent again, but only until husband Frederick died in 1914. The next year, she republished a serialized story, "Sunshine and Shadow or Paul Berton's Surprise," that had long before run in the local Edgerton paper. It may have been her last, for she passed away in 1920.

No less a literary figure than Mark Twain reveled in Moore's sweet singing, modeling the Emmeline Grangerford character on her in *Huckleberry Finn*. The twentieth century's comic poet Ogden Nash found her inspirational. Both humorists, they apparently took pleasure in her work regardless of the quality of the verse. The *Oxford Companion to American Literature* concurs; the poetry, it judges, was "so bad that it seemed to possess almost a touch of genius" with "unconsciously childish grammar, and rhymes that went from verse to worse."[8] The online *Literary Encyclopedia* gives her an elevated rank as "perhaps the most famous bad poet in the history of American literature." It also regarded her as representative of a now-forgotten genre: "As her poems frequently deal with death, she is often described as a 'mortuary poet,'

This is perhaps the only photograph of Julia Ann Moore, Michigan's "sweet singer." Papers of the Bibliographical Society of America, vol. 39, 111. Courtesy of Grand Rapids History and Special Collections, Archives, Grand Rapids Public Library, Grand Rapids, Michigan.

a name sometimes given to mediocre writers who dwell on the uncertainty of life in the nineteenth century."[9]

The Stuffed Owl: An Anthology of Bad Verse, first published in 1930, was reprinted in 2003 with an introduction by the U.S. poet laureate Billy Collins. Works by dozens of poets, the names of whom are unfamiliar to all but the most dedicated English Lit scholar, fill the volume, including Moore's. One also finds, however, a long list of the well-known, including John Dryden, Oliver Goldsmith, Robert Burns, Lord Byron, William Wordsworth, John Keats, Ralph Waldo Emerson, Edgar Allan Poe, Elizabeth Barrett Browning, and Henry Wadsworth Longfellow.

Moore never imagined her work would draw such attention, the original purpose being merely to entertain friends. She admitted that it needed seasoning. Defending its value, she pointed out that her writing came straight from the heart:

> There are two different fountains from whence inspiration flows to the writer, the intellect and the heart, the thought and feeling. Thought makes the best artist, has greater forethought, a wiser command of means, gives greater completeness, higher finish. But the heart has power *even* greater than this; a power of life and

soul, swaying the entire human sympathy and action. It has more freshness, more originality, more sincerity. Its highest influence is more enduring.

According to one academic critic, a professor of American literature at the University of Chicago, the Michigan poet fit squarely in the mainstream of American thought:

In Mrs. Moore's distinction between the poetry of the mind and poetry of the heart, we find a popularization of the romantic philosophy so gallantly espoused in England by Wordsworth, Coleridge, and their followers, and in America by the Transcendentalists. It was exactly the sort of an adaptation one would expect from average Americans, who memorized Poor Richard's Almanac, who were spurred to revolution by a pamphlet called Common Sense, and who always put kindness of intention and natural philosophy above "book l'arning."[10]

That Moore continued to be identified as the "sweet singer," given the dark themes she treated and her sometimes crude structure and form, may be attributed to one of two causes: either a fresh and unjaundiced approach to her best work, or its beneficial use as a means of coping light-heartedly during the most awful of times. She entertained, whether her poems were so bad as to be good, or she too innocent to understand high art. Regardless, she was guided by an open heart.

Julia Moore wrote poems some regard as works of genius, others as bad pop-song lyrics. The more contemporary Michigan poet Edgar A. Guest authored popular work in a genius all his own. The two had some things in common:

When a little baby dies
And the wee form silent lies,
And the little cheeks seem waxen
And the little hands are still,
Then your soul gives way to treason,
And you cry: "O, God, what reason,
O, what justice and what mercy
Have You shown us by Your will?"[11]

Guest obviously could write mortuary verse, a style no longer as popular.

He also wrote in words that find resonance today. In the early twenty-first century, one of the "Big Three" auto companies relied on Guest, and a sturdy, deep, earthy voice-over, to create a resolute image for the Chrysler 300 model motor vehicle:

When you're up against a trouble,
Meet it squarely, face to face;
Lift your chin and set your shoulders,
Plant your feet and take a brace.
When it's vain to try to dodge it,
Do the best that you can do;
You may fail, but you may conquer,
See it through!

Born in the English industrial hub of Birmingham in 1881, Guest emigrated to America at age ten with his financially strapped parents. They settled in Detroit because it was an uncle's home. The boy devoted himself to school for a short interval, but was forced to work when his father went jobless. While employed as a soda jerk, he confessed his real ambition—getting into the newspaper business—to a customer who happened to be an accountant at the *Detroit Free Press*. "Eddie" promptly got a summer job as an office boy in the bookkeeping department at $1.50 per week. He was fourteen and would be on the *Free Press* rolls for the next sixty-five years.

Guest advanced to cub reporter covering the nascent labor-union movement, marine writer, police reporter, and then exchange editor. In 1898, an assignment on the exchange desk, where filler verse and feature items were clipped for reprinting, led the seventeen-year-old to submit a few of his poems to the Sunday editor. The first appeared on December 11, under his byline. His efforts began to appear more frequently in the next few years. In 1904, the paper began regularly printing a column of his verse and observations, entitled "Chaff," then retitled "Blue Monday Chat."

During those early years at the *Free Press*, his pay barely supported subsistence. Reporters would frequent the cafés and lunch wagons on Lafayette between the paper's home and City Hall. John Colquhoun drew up his horse-drawn cart there, and Guest was a regular patron. So was an engineer for the electric utility, who spent evenings tinkering with an invention in his Bagley Avenue garage, emerging sometimes to find a late-night snack at Colquhoun's. Guest and Henry Ford became acquainted, then friends, and their pre-fame relationship would later motivate the auto czar to acquire the wagon for his history park, memorializing forever their humble beginnings together.[12]

Originally a weekly feature, Guest's writing grew steadily in popularity until the paper moved it to a daily column. By 1908, "the Poet of the People" as he became known, focused almost completely on the verse form. Beginning in 1916, "Edgar A. Guest's Breakfast Table Chat" was syndicated to some three hundred newspapers, and he was earning over $100,000 a year from the column and its spinoffs: books, greeting cards, calendars, radio appearances, and speaking engagements. In the 1930s Detroit began to hold an "Eddie Guest Day." His verse would appear in twenty published volumes, earning him honorary degrees from Muskingum College, Wayne State University, and the University of Michigan.

A modern sage terms Guest "the most famous poet in American history." He certainly was one of the ablest sellers. The same critic assesses that few today even know his name[13] despite the Chrysler commercial. Guest's use of blue-collar dialect marked by folksy abbreviations and contractions, according to Robert Pinsky, won immense popularity with his readership while he was alive; the same retrospective style is today an impediment to an ear attuned to imagination, surprise, and evocative imagery. Guest, on the other hand, is "still with us," unlike others whose work is completely forgotten. He was an expert at devising a style that resonated with his readership, then and now.

Contemporary readers were interested in "God, country, family, and home." Guest specialized in sentimentality, and the public loved it. *A Heap o' Livin',* issued in 1916, sold more than a million copies and is his most familiar poem. In 1988 he was voted into the Michigan Journalism Hall of Fame because "for more than 30 years there wasn't a *Free Press* that didn't carry his verse." This for a writer who confessed he was "a newspaperman who wrote verses."

Other critics, such as *Look Homeward, Angel*'s Thomas Wolfe, had less stomach for his homespun homilies. Wolfe derided that "sugary, sticky, sickening Edgar A. Guest sentimentality."[14] A more recent judgment in the

Lemony Snicket series is similar: "He was a writer of limited skill, who wrote awkward, tedious poetry on hopelessly sentimental topics."[15] Guest's poetry may have been sappy, but Michiganders oppressed by gloom could escape through it, for a moment at least.

Guest may have relied on the nostalgic, but his vision was not only rearward. On May 4, 1922, from a studio located on the ninth floor of the *Free Press* Building, radio station WCX transmitted its first broadcast. Ushering in the advent of this second Detroit over-the-air outlet, Governor Alexander Groesbeck and University of Michigan president Marion Burton addressed the sparse listening audience while Guest recited verse with his son, Edgar Jr. ("Bud"), at his side. The elder would soon have his own program at WCX, later becoming the "Great Voice" of WJR—as would Bud from 1946 until retirement in 1972. The junior Guest's "Sunny Side of the Street" echoed his father's style.

Another Guest family member would make their name familiar again late in the century. Great-niece Judith became a successful novelist with her most famous work, *Ordinary People*, published in 1976 and made into a motion picture in 1980 that won numerous awards.

Thus the arc makes a complete circle. Julia Moore's first popular work appeared exactly a century before Judith's. Ordinary people were her subject as they were for Edgar Guest Sr. In "He Who Serves," Guest devised a paean to the ordinarily unrecognized:

> He has not served who gathers gold,
> Nor has he served, whose life is told
> In selfish battles he has won,
> Or deeds of skill that he has done;
> But he has served who now and then
> Has helped along his fellow men.
>
> The world needs many men today;
> Red-blooded men along life's way,
> With cheerful smiles and helping hands,
> And with the faith that understands
> The beauty of the simple deed
> Which serves another's hour of need.

Strong men to stand beside the weak,
Kind men to hear what others speak;
True men to keep our country's laws
And guard its honor and its cause;
Men who will bravely play life's game
Nor ask rewards of gold and fame.

Teach me to do the best I can
To help and cheer our fellow man;
Teach me to lose my selfish need
And glory in the larger deed
Which smoothes the road, and lights the day
For all who chance to come my way.

An ordinary man himself, he left behind an extraordinary body of work. According to publishing giant John S. Knight, "very early, Eddie Guest discerned a fundamental truth about what people liked to read." And he gave it to them.

Very early, Guest did something else. At the beginning of his scrapbook, left behind for the world to see, are three shocking poems. Each begins with the "n" word—yes, *that* word. They feature stereotypical dialogue for the era, and each is from the viewpoint of the rather ill-educated narrator of African descent. Given the times, with Jim Crow and *Plessy v. Ferguson* and vaudeville acts in blackface, they seem almost mainstream. Looking at them with twenty-first-century eyes, one cannot help but cringe to think that Guest, eventually to become the people's poet, betrayed a huge segment of the population. We can judge him a century later to be, therefore—like the rest of his work—merely mortal.

But there's more. On one left-hand page of the volume is pasted Rudyard Kipling's famous "The White Man's Burden," a poem singing the praises of the British Empire and its white-supremacist mission of civilizing the Third World. Could Guest actually have identified with that message in these three early efforts? The answer is across the page, under the identical title, with Guest's own slants:

We've taken the White Man's burden,
We've sent forth the best we breed;
Our sons are bound to exile
To feed our selfish greed
They fought in heavy harness,
In foreign lands and wild;
We beat those sullen peoples,
Half devil and half child.

We've taken the White Man's burden,
And reaped his old reward;
The death of those who love us,
The death of those who guard
The cry of hosts we humor,
(Ah, slowly!) toward light—
"Why bought ye us of the Spaniards,
The people we could fight?"

We've taken the White Man's burden,
And now we have to fight;
We've got to kill the heathen
To put them in the right.
We have to lose our heroes,
Who give their lives and time
To raise that sullen people
Above ignorance and crime.

We've taken the White Man's burden,
We've done with childish days;
They scorned our proffered laurel,
They did not like our ways;
And so we had to kill them,
For we had to have that land;
No matter how much life it takes,
Our empire must expand.

The sweet sap came later. Here, only the acrid flowed. But for both poets, their rhymes were helpful to readership coping with the temporary ugliness of life in a green and pleasant land.

Works

JULIA ANN MOORE

The Sentimental Song Book (Grand Rapids, MI: C. M. Loomis, 1876).

The Sentimental Song Book: With Numerous Additions and Corrections by the Author (Cleveland: J. F. Ryder, 1877).

The Sweet Singer of Michigan: Later Poems of Julia A. Moore, Together with Reviews, Commendatory Notices, Etc., Etc., of Her Sentimental Song Book (Grand Rapids, MI: Eaton, Lyon & Co., 1878).

Sunshine and Shadow or Paul Berton's Surprise: A Romance of the American Revolution (Cadillac, MI: N.p., 1915).

EDGAR ALBERT GUEST

Home Rhymes (Detroit: H. R. Guest, 1909).

Breakfast Table Chat (Detroit: N.p., 1914).

Just Glad Tidings (Detroit: N.p., 1916).

A Heap o' Livin' (Chicago: Reilly and Lee, 1916).

Just Folks (Chicago: Reilly and Lee, 1917).

Over Here (Chicago: Reilly and Lee, 1918); reissued as *Poems of Patriotism* (Chicago: Reilly and Lee, 1922).

The Path to Home (Chicago: Reilly and Lee, 1919).

Sunny Songs (London: T. F. Unwin, 1920).

A Dozen New Poems (Chicago: Reilly and Lee, 1920).

When Day Is Done (Chicago: Reilly and Lee, 1921).

All That Matters (Chicago: Reilly and Lee, 1922).

The Passing Throng (Chicago: Reilly and Lee, 1923).

Rhymes of Childhood (Chicago: Reilly and Lee, 1924).

Mother (Chicago: Reilly and Lee, 1925).

The Light of Faith (Chicago: Reilly and Lee, 1926).

You (Chicago: Reilly and Lee, 1927).

Harbor Lights of Home (Chicago: Reilly and Lee, 1928).

Poems for the Home Folks (Chicago: Reilly and Lee, 1930).

The Friendly Way (Chicago: Reilly and Lee, 1931).

Picture-poems (St. Paul, MN: Brown and Bigelow, 1931).

Selected Poems by Edgar A. Guest, Radio Station WIBO (Chicago: J. Thomas, 1931).

Life's Highway (Chicago: Reilly and Lee, 1933).

Collected Verse of Edgar Guest (Chicago: Reilly and Lee, 1934).

All in a Life-time (Chicago: Reilly and Lee, 1938).

Between You and Me: My Philosophy of Life (Chicago: Reilly and Lee, 1938).

Today and Tomorrow (Chicago: Reilly and Lee, 1942).

Living the Years (Chicago: Reilly and Lee, 1949).

Sites

. . . .

JULIA ANN MOORE

Algoma Township (which prides itself today as the "Fields of Wild Roses")

Grave in Liberty Cemetery, North 41 Road, Manton, Wexford County

EDGAR ALBERT GUEST

Owl Night Lunch Wagon, Greenfield Village, The Henry Ford, Dearborn

Detroit Free Press Building, 321 W. Lafayette Street, Detroit

Grave in Woodlawn Cemetery, Detroit; Plot: Section 27, Lot 51, Grave 7

Arnold Mulder

Dutch Americans and Dunes

November 12, 1885–March 27, 1959

Born and lived most of his life in Michigan and used west Michigan as a fictional stage

. . . .

Few people . . . seem to realize that the dunes along Lake Michigan are as effective a background for fiction as the woods were at one time. I have felt for years that here is a region that in romantic interest is second to none.—ARNOLD MULDER, "Michigan as a Field for the Novelist"

When Arnold Mulder penned these words in 1922, he was either being modest or hinting that the reader should pick up a copy of his recent novel, The Sand Doctor. Mulder had attempted what he suggested other authors should do: capitalizing on the majesty of west Michigan's sand dunes to tell a story of human transience. The dunes are "beautiful with the unconscious artistry of a million years of sun and storm," he wrote in the novel.

The journey from his childhood to champion of the dunes was a winding one; a keen observer of the Dutch American community and religious organizations in and around Holland, Michigan, he ultimately pursued a secular theme in his final novel.

The twelfth of fifteen children born to first-generation Dutch immigrants on a farm in Holland Township, Mulder early on dreamed of becoming a famous novelist. At the age of twelve, he produced a fledgling:

a romance novel set during the War of 1812. Like most adolescent writings, it never found a publisher, but it expressed a yearning to create.

Steeped in a profoundly religious family, the boy turned man would gaze upon his faith and the community that cultivated it as the raw material of his early published fiction. It is impossible to separate Mulder from the conflict between the Reformed Church of America (RCA) and the Christian Reformed Church (CRC). His parents converted from the more liberal former to the latter, which adhered to Calvinist thought. In doing so, they provided Mulder with a window into two overlapping worlds.

The conflict dated back almost to the arrival of the first wave of immigrants from the Netherlands in 1847. Persecuted by the Dutch government for resisting the liberalization of the Dutch Reformed Church, and seeking economic opportunity, the Reverend Albertus Van Raalte and followers ended up in Michigan Territory almost by chance, foregoing their original Wisconsin destination thanks to an early winter that stopped their Great Lakes journey at Detroit. From there, Michigan boosters and the availability of suitable land in Ottawa County did the rest of the work. Van Raalte's flock began building its own Holland in Michigan.

Van Raalte urged the Dutch to stick to their community. In a letter to a Dutch businessman he hoped to lure to Holland, Michigan. Van Raalte wrote, "Americans are disposed to despise Hollanders, and we Hollanders naturally become embittered against them because of their cold selfishness. They may approach us with bold flatteries, but in reality they are after our money and influence. Yes, they actually despise us. They take us for a dull, slow, uncultured people, and boldly boast of their own superior intelligence … I thank God that I may live in the midst of my own people." It was against a backdrop of Dutch American resistance to assimilation that Mulder cast his first stories.

The omnipresence of faith in the Dutch community demonstrated itself in small towns through the abundance of Reformed and Christian Reformed congregations. Their differing points of view were hard to miss: the houses of worship sometimes faced each other from opposite sides of the street.

Although raised in the Christian Reformed Church, Mulder graduated from Hope College, an RCA school, in 1907. He worked at the *Holland City News* for two years before enrolling at the University of Michigan and, after

Arnold Mulder depicted the challenges of Dutch Americans assimilating into American culture in the Holland area. He also authored a novel set against the dunes of Lake Michigan and was a nationally known book critic. Courtesy of the Kalamazoo College Archives.

a semester in Ann Arbor, the University of Chicago, receiving a master's degree in English literature in 1910. Life in these profoundly American communities, swirling with liberal thought, further sharpened the young author's perspective on the immigrant community of the Holland area.

Mulder returned to Holland after college to wed his sweetheart of six years, Kathryn Kollen. He paid the bills by serving as editor of the *Holland Sentinel*, a competitor of his former newspaper. He settled in town with his wife, the niece of Hope College's president, and began work on his first novel.

The Dominie of Harlem, published in 1913, was reviewed and generally praised nationally, one reviewer calling it a remarkable debut. In Holland, reaction was mixed. Some condemned it for mocking the Christian Reformed Church and its adherents.

The central character of *The Dominie of Harlem* is Dominie (pastor) van Weelen, a young minister who brings fresh energy and liberal ways to Harlem, a thinly disguised Holland. Not part of the chronic dueling between the RCA and CRC, van Weelen is free to dispense modern wisdom to congregants, including the Harmdyk family. Harmdyk patriarch Jan, a widower, struggles to raise his children and keep them pious. By showing kindness and tending to the Harmdyk offspring, the pastor opens their eyes to a new way of expressing faith and ultimately wins the eldest son, Ezra, back from blasphemy while charming daughter Nellie into marriage.

The message of modernization is clear. It was not unanimously welcomed in the Dutch community. A reviewer for a periodical of the CRC commented that "an author also must reckon with Him who entrusted talents, including literary talents—to uplift, to ennoble, but not to deal unjustly with any man or set of men."

In 1915, Mulder left journalism to become publicity director for the Michigan State Health Commission. The same year, he published his second novel, *Bram of the Five Corners*. This time the conflict between the ways of the immigrant community and those of secular America was illustrated by the two women in Bram's love life, simple villager and fiancée Hattie, and Cordelia, an outsider who moves to Five Corners from Chicago. Neither is satisfactory to Bram, the former because she has limited horizons and the latter because she cannot understand the Dutch and their ways.

Feeling smothered by family and community expectations that he pursue the ministry, Bram instead chooses the secular route of newspaper reporting with a missionary bent. He is attacked by local Calvinists for abandoning his true calling. Likewise, Mulder's traditionalist peers in Holland criticized the novel for oversimplifying the doctrine and practices of the conservatives.

In one scene illustrative of the clash of Dutch faiths, a worshiper is astonished to hear his liberal RCA minister preaching "evolootion." The six days the Bible says it took God to fashion creation, the minister says, are actually six periods of millions of years each. "You mean to say that God did not create the heavens and the earth, as it says plain in the Bible, in six days of twenty-four hours each?" the congregant asks. When the pastor affirms the statement, the worshiper hotly tells him he will leave the church to attend the CRC: "there at least they preach no evolootion."

His next book appeared in 1919. Mulder's third and final novel exploring Dutch American themes, *The Outbound Road* incorporates but transcends Mulder's familiar story line of the Dutch immigrant descent into the American melting pot. Its narrator is a faculty member of a school not unlike Hope College, but its chief protagonist is the adopted son of a Polish American actress, born out of wedlock. He has a very different destiny, far beyond west Michigan, from what his parents envision.

Named Teunis by his adoptive Dutch American parents, the boy—and young man he becomes—instinctively bridles at the family strictures. In one pivotal incident, the little boy manages to scrape together enough money to go to the county fair, where he jumps onstage and amuses the crowd. Shocked by his son's disobedience, but even more by his love of the "scandalous" county fair, the father, Foppe Spykhoven, imposes a humiliating judgment, which nevertheless fails to discourage Teunis's dreams of exploring the wider world.

Mulder's rendering of the old man's worldview is affectionate, not harsh. His love of a child he never expected to have balances his discipline. Meanwhile, the boy's vivid imagination is described amusingly after his father observes that Satan may get the upper hand on the lad.

> Teunis's mental picture of Satan was taken bodily from the Dutch version of *Pilgrim's Progress*. The hoofs and tails and horns stood out prominently. It appeared from the picture in the book that Christian had got the best of this most interesting adversary; and Teunis had enough of an instinctive belief in his own vitality to feel confident that what another had done he could do. He sensed the dramatic possibilities of an encounter with his satanic majesty, and instead of his father's warning giving him pause, it made him prick up his mental ears. Possibly, after all, there might be something to live for!

Teunis makes no secret of his impatience with community mores. Urged by Christian College fathers to apologize for being caught drinking at a dance club and to renounce his sinful ways, Teunis instead shocks them and says the school president should go to hell. He then disappears from town, traveling widely in search of an outlet for his artistic talents. When he returns for a time to work a farm job that puts him pleasurably in touch with the soil, the local newspapers ridicule him. After further embarrassments, he departs again and wins fame as a major dramatist.

The book's narrator unflinchingly defends Teunis's unconventional journey. "The world thinks he's a failure, but he isn't. He has been true to his best instincts. And because those instincts led him out of the ordinary humdrum grooves, on to the outbound road, he has suffered."

At novel's end, Teunis and his aged father are reconciled, respecting their differences. Neither will "desert his own ideals, far apart as the poles, but the new-found understanding that each reads in the eyes of the other, and which is but another name for the love of one strong man for another, will bridge the gulf." Mulder himself has resolved his conflict. The Dutch community could retain its identity *and* thrive as a contributing member of American society. He would not return to the theme.

Scholar George Fuller said, "*The Outbound Road* will live for its human value long after very much of contemporary fiction is forgotten. . . . The secret of its power is its author's ability to see the universal values in the commonplace, and his possession of a keen sense of dramatic value."

Mulder returned to his Holland newspaper job after two years with the State Health Commission. In 1921, he published what would prove to be his final novel, *The Sand Doctor*.

The protagonist is young physician Briar Quentin, who meets his wife-to-be, Hallie, in the Lake Michigan dunes. Hallie encourages her young husband to expand his practice by conforming to the expectations of their small town. But Briar has no use for this. He would rather tramp the dunes and study their geology than pretend to enjoy glad-handing and humoring hypochondriacal, if wealthy, patients.

The difference in values cleaves the once-romantic couple. A peculiar character with a split personality, Barry Larramore, enters the scene. As the result of an accident, Barry has divided into a solemn, practical business-man on the one hand and a happy-go-lucky youth on the other. In spite of herself, Hallie grows fond of the young Barry, while Briar considers the man a fascinating psychological case whom he hopes to cure.

In a dramatic finale, Briar's disdain for moneymaking is proven to be warranted and he is successful in surgery to heal Barry. But a severe storm nearly buries Briar in dune sand. After a fortuitous rescue, husband and wife are happily reunited, and rekindle their romance in the same dunes where they met.

"Men deluded themselves with the thought that they were its masters," Briar thinks. "But the sand paid no heed. It bided its time, and then it impersonally overwhelmed everything in its path. It crept down upon its prey grain by grain in the slow years. It could afford to take its time. A thousand years were but as a second in the span of its life. If it did not overwhelm a victim to-day it would a century hence . . . It was mighty! It was splendid!"

Reaction to *The Sand Doctor* was sharply divided. The *Nation* said Mulder had gone "badly to pieces." Closer to home, *Michigan History* magazine applauded the author for seizing "upon the romantic and picturesque features of these shifting sands and fascinat[ing] us with his love of them as others have charmed us with their love of the mountains and the sea. His power and versatility in describing the dunes is noteworthy."

It is unclear why Mulder abandoned fiction after *The Sand Doctor*. He lived another thirty-eight years, serving as professor at Kalamazoo College until retirement. He authored magazine articles and literary criticism. He also wrote two nonfiction volumes, one about the Dutch in America and one about the college.

As a critic, Mulder railed against snobbery:

The classification of books as "serious books and fiction" is ridiculous, reminiscent of the days when it was still considered immoral to read novels. We have become ashamed of that point of view as narrow-minded, and so a large number of people have shifted from the moral to the intellectual tack in their opposition to works of fiction. Reading should improve the mind, they hold, and hence people should be encouraged to read "serious" books and to let novels alone. As if a fact set down by a dull mind is more serious and has greater potentiality for mental improvement than a subtle observation drawn by a genius from the laboratory of real life and in which he distills in a sentence the wisdom of a generation.

More than once, Mulder contemplated and wrote of Michigan's literary history and potential as a setting for the novelist. Mulder analyzed the record of Michigan writers in a March 1939 issue of the *Saturday Review of Literature*. His article was entitled "Authors and Wolverines: The Books and Writers of Michigan."

Citing efforts of tourism boosters to offer up Michigan as the home of celebrated authors, Mulder retorted, "But sober honesty compels the admission that Authors—upper case Authors—are about as rare in Michigan as the 'skunk bear' [wolverine] ever was and that the flowering of literary Michigan is still in the future." On the other hand, he said, Michigan did not lack literary fodder.

> The fiction writer is reduced to looking for his effects in slow mass movements, transitions lacking in "theater," the displacement of the lumber man by the farmer and of the farmer by the assembly-line man in the automobile factory. Such themes are too promising to be neglected. And behind the physical drama of lumber—the log-jams and sawmill camps often treated in fiction—there is an even more highly exciting economic and political drama, which is largely untouched.

In the three-quarters of a century since Mulder issued this assessment, his own decade-long burst of creativity has receded into obscurity. Yet he was a pioneer: one of the first Dutch American novelists, and the first to depict the dunes of Lake Michigan so lovingly. There is something worth salvaging from his works. He recorded a critical time in the assimilation of the Dutch of west Michigan—and celebrated for the first time in fiction the immutable beauty of the restless dunes of the Lake Michigan shoreline.

Works

The Dominie of Harlem (Chicago: A.C. McClurg and Co., 1913).
Bram of the Five Corners (Chicago: A.C. McClurg and Co., 1915).
The Outbound Road (Boston: Houghton Mifflin Co., 1919).
The Sand Doctor (Boston: Houghton Mifflin Co., 1921).
Americans from Holland (Philadelphia: J.B. Lippincott, 1948).
The Kalamazoo College Story: The First Quarter of the Second Century of Progress, 1933–1958 (Kalamazoo, MI: Kalamazoo College, 1958).

Sites

Mt. Pisgah, Historic Ottawa Beach Park, adjacent to Holland State Park, Holland
Pilgrim Home Cemetery, Holland, Plot PH1/WE/47.7

John Tobin Nevill

Unlikely Yooper

July 11, 1901–July 14, 1957

Lived and worked in Detroit; lived in and wrote from De Tour

Mention "cynical" or "jaded," and "newspapermen" comes immediately to mind. They've seen the worst of humanity and made a career out of writing about it. Before long, they come to expect the worst and are rarely disappointed.

Jack Nevill knew and wrote much about the vagaries of life. Born in Texas, he was seventh of eight children of a Texas Ranger who faced gangs of outlaws. Charles Nevill joined the troop at age nineteen, fought Apaches, arrested a notorious train robber named Sam Bass, broke up the Jesse Evans Gang, and helped capture the Potter Gang. Rewarding his exploits, the people of Presidio County in the Trans-Pecos territory of west Texas elected him sheriff. Bordering the Rio Grande, it is arid land interrupted only by cacti and ocotillos. The county was the suitable setting for the 1959 John Wayne/Howard Hawks classic *Rio Bravo*, a tale of brutality and heroism. Charles died at age fifty-one, his passing no doubt precipitated by a hard life. Jack was not yet five; he wasn't yet fourteen when his mother died.

At sixteen he aided the remaining family fortunes by enlisting in the Marines. His duty stations included Europe, Turkey, the West Indies, and South America aboard a battleship, the USS *Arizona*, that one day would be known around the world. After being discharged, he crossed over the Big Bend to work in the Mexican oil fields. It was hard labor, and he looked for an easier occupation, which turned out to be writing for a small-town Texas newspaper. After a couple of years at the *Greenville Evening Banner* northeast of Dallas, he sought a larger stage and tried his luck in the Big Apple. Unable to land a reporting job in Manhattan, he ended up in construction. The early days of flight opened the doors to his first professional publication. *Aviation* magazine published a number of his freelance pieces during the 1920s; he "enjoyed some distinction as the last newsman to fly on any air tour trip: he went along on the last, futile Pathfinder trip of 1932."[1] Edsel Ford, only son of the car company founder, had taken up the cause of promoting aviation advancements by lending his name to a trophy for the annual "National Air Tour." The trip in which Nevill participated lasted only a few days, thanks to financial difficulty caused by the Great Depression.

Perhaps that Ford connection is what landed him in the Motor City. On October 9, 1928, he and Margaret Ann (Peggy) Collins of London, England, were wed in Detroit. He was now a reporter for the *Detroit Free Press*, following stints at the *Detroit Times* and as a contributor to wire services such as United Press International. By the century's midpoint he was in public relations for the auto industry as it roared out of World War II and put the nation on wheels. In August 1950, having traveled to all forty-eight states on publicity work, he, Peggy, and daughter Sally Kathleen set off from their home at 5818 Eastlawn, just east of Chandler Park in Detroit, to explore northern Michigan. The trip would prove life-changing.

This vacation to the Upper Peninsula was to be a two-week respite from "the nerve-destroying chore of operating an advertising and public-relations office in Detroit." The family drove to Mackinaw City, took the ferry across the Straits to St. Ignace, and drove up US-2 toward Sault Ste. Marie. At M-134, the first major intersection with an easterly road, they happened to make a right turn, unlike most tourists. The unpaved route took them through Hessel and Cedarville, forty-four miles of scenery and sparse settlement, and to the end of the road and another ferry crossing to remote

John Tobin Nevill, a hard-boiled reporter, fell in love with the eastern Upper Peninsula and coauthored the first book on the "Mighty Mac."

Drummond Island. At this eastern terminus of the Upper Peninsula, they made a discovery.

Nevill was set to return to a high-powered job in thriving Detroit in an era when the city was at the apogee of population and power. He didn't hunt, didn't fish. He was amenable, however, to the influence of startling natural beauty:

> We were shown the St. Mary's River where it widens into island-studded Potagan-nissing Bay just above Drummond Island, and most important of all, we were shown a spot on the river's mainland side where tall timber—spruce, cedar, and balsam, sprinkled with a condiment of birch and poplar, and a few maples—lined the shore almost to the water's edge. There was a sandy beach, and just a couple of stone's throws out in the river were the boat channels, where large ore-carriers glided by seemingly endlessly.

This end of the road was aptly named De Tour. Just a village, its history ranged back to the fur traders and beyond. Its French name meant "the

LES CHENEAUX ISLANDS

This bird's-eye view of the east end of the Upper Peninsula features the glacially distinct Les Cheneaux archipelago. Courtesy of the Clarke Historical Library, Central Michigan University.

turn,"[2] similar to the Ojibway name "Giwideonaning," the "point which we go around in a canoe."

Here, "at the mouth of the twisting and inspirationally scenic St. Mary's River," the Nevills decided to go round no farther, to take to the wilderness, to make this—not "De Troit"—home. They located a property at Spring Bay, on the road by that name, four miles north of De Tour and built a house, leaving behind "feverish, noisy, industry-crowded Detroit."

When friends and business associates back in southeast Michigan questioned this impulsive decision, Nevill had a ready explanation:

It's the huge orange-colored sun sinking into gold-splashed water between two Les Cheneaux islands. It's the purple, and lavender, and gold, and blue, and white blended so beautifully in the clouds hanging low over Potagannissing Bay in the late afternoon. It's the deep-throated whistles of two ore-carriers saying "hello" as they pass one another. It's the highlands of St. Joe Island, blue in the distance, as seen from our living room. It's the *pum-pum-pum* of a diesel-powered vessel passing in the night, or the gentle slapping of waves on our beach . . . It's the exquisite comfort of lying, snug and warm in bed on a winter night, and listening to icy winds whistling through the tall evergreens outside our windows. It's the snow piled high atop our roof, and the long icicles forming a silver portiere outside our picture windows, while we sit in shirt-sleeved comfort before an open fireplace inside . . . It's the soothing quiet of early morning, with "steam" hovering over the cold lake water. It's the cool, invigorating air one can almost bite off in chunks.

Yes, one could watch ore carriers along the Huron side of Michigan, "but who, in his right mind, would compare the relatively narrow, oil-smeared, industry-choked Detroit River with a majestic stream like the St. Mary's?"

The main issue was how to make a living here. He was forty-nine and far from retirement. The 1950 Census counted just over six hundred De Tour inhabitants, no thriving newspapers, and little need for a public relations man. But Nevill went back to freelancing, offering vignettes and stories overheard from locals to the *Evening News* of Sault Ste. Marie. Their irregular but ongoing appearances won him enough followers to land a regular job as feature writer. His columns added a new voice: mainstream U.P. literature, from Hemingway to Traver, had centered on locales west of the Soo highway. The eastern arrowhead had been overlooked, though a glance at the map showed it to be a gross oversight. Jutting into Lake Huron, this part of the Upper Peninsula featured the Les Cheneaux archipelago, historic Lime Island, and a host of evocative place names such as Caribou and Big Trout Lakes, St. Vital and Munuscong Bays. De Tour had gained distinction as a busy base of operations for lumbermen and anglers, the rocky waters littered with more sunken vessels per linear foot of frontage than any other Great Lakes port. For that reason, it became home to an iconic feature of the Great Lakes State. Beginning in 1848, a shoreline lighthouse guided sailors to safety at the mouth of the St. Marys where it empties Lake Superior into Lake Huron. The 1930s construction of a reef light one mile out in the channel aimed to prevent more disasters.

Nevill readily made the transition from Detroiter to Yooper—a term of endearment fashioned out of the two letters abbreviating the Upper Peninsula. Within the first year he was poking at the Motor City for overzealous pride in its ancient history:

So Detroit is preparing to celebrate its 250th birthday? You'll have to pardon DeTour for greeting the news with a polite yawn. It's hard to impress this village that was visited by white men—Jesuit Fathers, Raymbouit and Jorues—in 1543. That was 158 years before Cadillac landed on the site of what is now Detroit . . . DeTour counts as comparative late visitors Fr. Marquette, who dropped in 1668, and La Salle, who was aboard the ill-fated vessel *Griffin* in 1679.

This column appeared under his byline as Free Press special writer, and the newcomer's enthusiasm for their place tickled his new neighbors. He chided snowbirds for fleeing two of the four seasons—why live here if you do not embrace fall and winter? The foreword to Nevill's first book hailed his embrace of the new home: "It took a Texan with an English-born wife to appreciate the flavor of the Northland." The words were penned by ex-congressman and then-chairman of the new Mackinac Bridge Authority, Prentiss M. Brown, with whom Nevill had formed a friendship. Most likely it was founded on their shared passion for Upper Michigan.

Nevill knew how to tell a story about local stuff. He devised a series of seventeen articles about the Seamans of Drummond Island, an extended family whose roots on the rock went back to 1853. He wrote a six-edition story of Aunt Jane Goudreau's dangerous time on Beaver Island during the Chicago Fire; she later moved to St. Ignace, where he heard her account. He wrote of people and places, of myths and tall tales, finding a lode of lore that was of great interest to the north country citizens.

Several years of columns were collected into *Wanderings: Sketches of Northern Michigan Yesterday and Today*, which appeared in hardback, copyrighted 1955. The publisher was Exposition Press, a leading vanity press firm operating out of New York.[3] Looking every bit as genuine as any publication,[4] the back jacket featured a photo of the author, wearing a plaid shirt in classic U.P. style, slicked gray hair, salt and pepper mustache, dark eyebrows, and rather heavy bags under his deep eyes. His smile, though, was the most striking aspect. The front cover contained an outline of Michigan and the surrounding Great Lakes, with progressive concentric rings emanating from the eastern tip of the Upper Peninsula. No other volume in print, surely, has placed the center of the universe at the eastern end of Michigan's northern peninsula.

The book covered the waterfront of personalities besides the serene places that had drawn him there. A pioneer Catholic priest nicknamed Iron Head made an appearance; Finn Charlie, a hermit, also merited inclusion. In one yarn, Henry Ford borrowed a nickel for a copy of the *News* while in the locks on a down-bound journey from the Huron Mountain Club. Embarrassed, he put his wife Clara up to asking a deckhand for the coin. Quacky Olmstead and Corny Ortago, Curly Lewis and Harto Hartwell—and similar such characters—demonstrated that the eastern Upper Peninsula was as fascinating as the western.

He also included a chapter on a bridge that "couldn't" be built between St. Ignace and the Lower Peninsula. Then under construction and two years from opening, the project inspired an idea for a second book. Cowritten with bridge designer David B. Steinman, making it a uniquely first-person account, *Miracle Bridge at Mackinac* was published in late 1957. The first full-length account of the seven-year-long, 100 million-dollar venture, it was part engineering journal, part historical record, part ode to the determination and perseverance of Michiganders. This time, the foreword was written by G. Mennen Williams, governor of Michigan and self-described "good friend" of Nevill.

Bridging the gap between the two major peninsulas would end the inevitable delays that motorists endured from taking a ferry to cross the Straits. At times, as in deer season, the wait could last hours. Uniting Michigan's halves conveniently, reliably, and safely had been a dream for many decades. In 1903, car ferry service was launched between Northport at the tip of the Leelanau peninsula and Manistique, thanks to the Manistique, Marquette & Northern Railroad, but service lasted only five years. Two decades later, ferry runs became regular across the 5-mile Mackinac Straits, an easier proposition than the earlier 65-mile journey. Nothing could be more like Michigan, though, than constructing a highway to join the peninsulas.

The *Miracle Bridge* coauthors prefaced their work with personal reflections on the project. Steinman naturally felt the pride of direct involvement as designer and supervisor. Nevill's ardor for the bridge stemmed from his sense of personal "ownership," arising out of "the pride which comes from being a resident of a great commonwealth which has shown the vision, and the wisdom, and the sheer temerity to build a structure such as this!" A year before, the two had sat together in an auto "on a rise of ground near Hessel" some twenty miles from the bridge, admiring the progress, congratulating each other on the looming achievement.

Before this audacious project had begun, other notions of how to link the two halves of Michigan had to be overcome. A generation before, the state highway commissioner advocated a floating tunnel across the Straits. Another creative mind suggested starting a procession of bridges and causeways near Cheboygan that would cross over to the Bois Blanc, Round, and Mackinac isles, ultimately connecting across to St. Ignace. Previous attempts at a bridge authority had failed. Legal counsel in that defeat, Nevill's friend and St. Ignace native Prentiss Brown became chief proponent of a new effort. The final decision to create a human-made isthmus across the gap challenged recent experience, such as the disastrous 1940 span collapse at Tacoma, Washington; waded into uncertain financial waters; but ultimately went forward, thanks to this "father of the bridge."[5] Thankfully, it did not transit through Mackinac Island, saving that purely Michigan site as the glorious auto-free destination it remains.

It might also not have been as beautiful or majestic. Steinman's design was grace itself. The double towers, symbolizing the two great peninsulas, featured three elegant, horizontal braces with three "X" piercings in each link, providing stylish detail. The U.S. Post Office issued a commemorative stamp within a year of completion, the two towers rising with simple beauty above the deep blue water as a classic laker, tiny by comparison, steams eastward underneath. This, the first of many such images, proved up the dream. Anything less dramatic would have disgraced Michigan. Today, the bridge's classic lines and established place in Michigan history—a central icon on so many symbols of Michigan, including the latest custom auto license plate— make it hard to imagine how exciting it was, and controversial, when proposed six decades ago. Designed to be timeless, the bridge perfectly fit the setting Nature's God fashioned for it.

The book's concluding chapter bravely bore the heading "The Meaning of Mackinac." Brave because not many would hasten to sum up a site and a project that challenges comprehension. Nevill's pen here clearly predominated:

The Upper Peninsula of Michigan—nearly seventeen thousand square miles of the most picturesque country to be found in North America—is the birthplace of Michigan, and therefore has always been a part of Michigan ...

Because of its natural charm and physical beauty, its invigorating climate, and the abundance of wildlife in its woods and waters, the Upper Peninsula contributes heavily to the state's eminent position among vacation and resort states of the Union. It has come to be known as a "Vacation Paradise." . . .

Since the 1840s, this magical "land of the sky-blue waters" has enjoyed a number of "boom eras"—copper, iron, lumber, and recreation. The Mackinac Bridge is certain to stimulate each of these, perhaps recreation the greatest of all. As one U.P. businessman put it when workmen began to assemble at the Straits to build the bridge: "This is the biggest thing that has happened to us since God put copper and iron in our soil, and then adorned that soil with the finest building timber known to man."

And *that* is the meaning of the "Miracle Bridge at Mackinac!"[6]

Man, unfortunately, had exhausted most of the mineral and timber wealth of the Upper Peninsula. Now, humanity was constructing a bridge to a more sustainable future.

The governor's piece talked of how Nevill's excitement—"no one in Michigan was prouder of the bridge"—prompted painstaking research and produced zealous description. Williams was proud, too, proclaiming that the bridge "is a true reflection of the spirit of Michigan." It was the same spirit that had driven Nevill to leave his city life behind: "adventurous, unafraid, alive always to the call of new frontiers." His friend had found new life here on the shore of Lake Huron and its contiguous waters. But another thing needed to be told about Jack Nevill in these introductory remarks. It was his tragic death.

Sunday morning, July 14, 1957, Peggy awoke to the smell of smoke. A blaze had broken out in the adjoining garage and now threatened to engulf the ranch house. She desperately sought to rouse her husband and together flee to safety. She found him insensate, apparently from the smoke. Trying futilely to pull him through a window after she had crawled through, Peggy was overcome, slowly regained consciousness, then desperately ran for help nearby. When she returned, the house was consumed by flames; it was too late. Her husband was found inside. The bridge manuscript, with finishing touches nearly completed, somehow survived. With terseness that the reporter himself would have used, newspapers recounted his tragic death at age fifty-five.

Steinman saw to the posthumous publication, crediting Nevill as a collaborator. Four months after the fatal fire, the span opened to traffic.

The Nevills had lived for only seven years in the Upper Peninsula, but it was long enough to gain him insight. His last written words predicted that the bridge would transform Michigan in terms of both commerce and tourism. Approaching six decades of operation now, without a single structural problem, the Mackinac Bridge remains a testament to determination and faith. Nevill embraced it, thought it a grand idea, and trumpeted its significance for his fellow Michiganders, both the trolls still living below the bridge and the north countrymen whose hardiness would not be diminished by its construction: "Given willpower enough, and brains enough, and faith enough, and money enough, virtually *anything* can be done."

De Tour is still at the terminus of M-134, alternatively known as North Huron Shore Drive and South Scenic Road. Interesting, this drive, winding through prototypical Michigan towns such as Cedarville; past Wilderness, Mackinac, and Beaver Tail Bays; beyond the lighthouse point, past where the ferry crosses to Drummond and the ore carriers and iron boats go down to Gary and Milwaukee and Detroit and on to the world. The 1931-vintage light station has been preserved, with a new Michigan historical marker dedicated in September 2013. The sign is located at the MDOT scenic parking area known as "Hot Dog Stands Beach," on M-134 five miles west of De Tour, where the lighthouse is first sighted from the roadway. Travelers have to traverse the magical bridge; they usually rush past the connection on Interstate 75, or turn off on US-2 toward the Cut River Bridge and Fayette ghost town and parts west. They would do well to follow a writer's example and instead head toward the rising sun.

"What I write is generally forgotten by tomorrow," said Nevill modestly in *Wanderings*. He wrote some funny pieces, some painful to read, many that made his readers remember the story long after they had forgotten the source. His love for the eastern tip of the Upper Peninsula deserves to be remembered.

Works

Wanderings: Sketches of Northern Michigan Yesterday and Today (New York: Exposition Press, 1955).

Miracle Bridge at Mackinac (with David B. Steinman) (Grand Rapids, MI: Wm. B. Eerdmans Publishing, 1957).

Sites

5818 Eastlawn, Detroit
Home site on Spring Bay
Rise (on M-134) in Hessel

Constance Maybury Rourke

An American Original

November 14, 1885–March 29, 1941
Grand Rapids was her base beginning at the age of two

Is there such a thing as American culture? The answer may seem obvious today, but for much of the nation's first 150 years, a debate raged over the question. Was American culture an inferior knockoff of Europe's rich heritage, or something original and worth studying and cherishing? Did popular culture—the myths of movies and detective novels—matter?

In the eyes of many, a Michigan-based scholar and author settled the matter. Obscure for decades, her reputation rebounded in 2004 with the reissuance of a classic piece of criticism introduced by the leading chronicler of rock-and-roll music. She is now considered one of the greats of American cultural interpretation.

Born in Cleveland, Constance Maybury Rourke was brought to Grand Rapids by her mother, Constance Davis Rourke, in the winter of 1888, less than a year after her father Henry's death. The formidable mother had defied her own parents by pursuing a teaching career and divorcing her first husband. Adoring, yet strict with her daughter, the elder Constance

Anchored in Grand Rapids most of her life, Constance Maybury Rourke traveled widely in search of documentation for her thesis that American culture had a vibrancy and originality that transcended its colonial roots. Her works are remembered as classics of criticism. Courtesy of Grand Rapids History and Special Collections, Archives, Grand Rapids Public Library, Grand Rapids, Michigan.

was a reformer who championed kindergarten in Grand Rapids and became a principal of the same school for twenty years. She organized evening courses for immigrants, steeping them in American ways.

A single working mother in a time when most adult women tended home fires, the elder Constance, perhaps toughened by her burdens, was not lavish with her emotions. A friend described her as "rather chary of expressed affection." She was considered authoritarian, even a tyrant in her profession. But she formed a loving, if tightly bound, attachment with the young Constance.

Her daughter's education was not left to chance. Constance was well-schooled, not only in conventional subjects but also in the arts, which provided an early foundation for her understanding of culture. Her mother influenced her deeply in other ways. The daughter is said to have once declared that she would marry, have a baby, and divorce by thirty-five, roughly echoing her mother's history. A biographer said young Constance's mother made her "an extension of herself, and . . . Constance knew at an early age that the route to maternal affection lay in acting solely as her mother's daughter."

After graduating from Grand Rapids Central High School in 1902, she enrolled at Vassar. Her mother apparently bankrolled her education, perhaps from an inheritance. Studying English, she made few friends and plunged into her studies. Professors who instilled an ethic of service impressed Constance, whose mother had also taught that social reform was a moral responsibility. One of her teachers, Gertrude Buck, advocated "social criticism," holding that what mattered was whether literature contributed to the life of the reader. The implication was that popular culture had value for both enjoyment and criticism.

Graduating from Vassar in 1907, Constance emerged with a stipend for travel in Europe, voted by her classmates. She deferred the trip in favor of a year of teaching in Grand Rapids. She then embarked for London with her mother. She visited English schools and examined social movements, later traveling to France, Germany, Switzerland, and Italy. After her mother returned home, a winter in Paris opened her eyes to modern art and music. The experience threatened to deflect her from teaching plans. She envisioned becoming a writer and a student of American culture.

At the same time that she began to depart from the career vision she had shared with her mother, she wrote her mother that Christmas 1909 would be their first and last apart. Although Constance accepted a teaching position at Vassar that would last until 1915, she remained tethered to her mother through almost daily correspondence. When the daughter quit her post, it was at least partly due to her mother's influence.

Ill health clouded her first years after returning to Grand Rapids. Teaching at a local high school, she began to submit articles to national publications. Her first major breakthrough was an essay on vaudeville, published in the *New Republic* in 1919. In 1920 the same publication used her essay on Paul Bunyan. The pattern was clear. She was moving from teacher to social critic.

She was entering a lively debate in the world of American letters. For more than a hundred years American artists had retreated to Europe to immerse themselves in an artistic environment their milieu was thought to lack. Before Twain, critics had argued that America lacked a native literature; after Twain, some doubted it could hold up when compared to the European oeuvre. More recently, some critics argued, the economic explosion of America had turned the arts crass and vulgar, with little to recommend them for study and appreciation. Rourke took the opposite view: that American mythmaking was proof of a distinctive and legitimate culture, and that just as the new nation had hewn a nascent civilization out of woods, waters, mountains, and prairie, its people had carved out of raw experience an emerging culture.

From 1920 to 1927, Rourke built a reputation as a reviewer. When her mother retired in 1924, the two shared a modest Grand Rapids home. But research took Constance away for extended periods, as did the writing of her first book, *Trumpets of Jubilee*, published in 1927.

The book is a study of five culturally influential nineteenth-century Americans: Henry Ward Beecher, Harriet Beecher Stowe, Lyman Beecher, Horace Greeley, and P. T. Barnum. The thread linking the five was their role in shaping an emerging American culture. Each was popular and thus excited Rourke's interest. She wrote:

> It is a habit these days to scorn popularity, and to measure successful leaders by their product, which may not always be exquisite. But popularity is a large gauge and a lively symbol; the popular leader is nothing less than the vicarious crowd, registering much that is essential and otherwise obscure in social history, hopes and joys and conflicts and aspirations which may be crude and transitory, but none the less are the stuff out of which the foundations of social life are made.

What others saw as vulgarity in Barnum was exactly what recommended him to Rourke. A showman who founded a circus and made riches by promoting hoaxes such as a mermaid with the head of a monkey and the tail of a fish, he was the perfect subject. Rourke contended that in a sense Barnum had no private life. "He lived in the midst of the crowd, in the peopled haunts of his great museum, on the road, on the lecture platform, on steamers, in caravans or circus trains, near the smell of sawdust or under the spreading lights of the city."

It was more than notoriety that stimulated the critic's interest in Barnum. The promoter "let play upon the faint stirrings of popular desires the energy of a sportive imagination, a fancy primitive but dramatic." The three-ring circus may have been his greatest achievement, the epitome of wonder: the fruits of a restive national imagination that Barnum had the power to divine.

Rourke had found her voice and her message: that the American character and the American experience were something wholly new, if traceable in part to traditions imported from other lands. The study of American culture was not only worthwhile but essential to an understanding of the nation. And it was the duty of one group of Americans to conduct and publicize the results of that study. In the closing of *American Humor*, she wrote, "The difficult task of discovering and diffusing the materials of the American tradition—many of them still buried—belongs for the most part to criticism."

Rourke's next book was *Troupers of the Gold Coast*, a biography of actress Lotta Crabtree. Dubbed "The Nation's Darling" during her heyday in the 1870s and 1880s, Crabtree roamed the nation and Europe to vast acclaim. Her earnings are said to have peaked at $5,000 a week in the 1880s. As one of the first celebrities of her kind, Crabtree marked a turning point in American culture. Managed by her own mother and never married, Crabtree lived a personal life parallel to Rourke's. She was a celebrity before the term was in vogue.

Rourke's next work after that may have been her most important. *American Humor: A Study of the National Character* powerfully makes the case that America began to express and identify itself through humor. She identifies the backwoodsman, blackface performer, and Yankee peddler as early and original archetypes of humor, both serving as, and generating the jokes of an America developing in the early 1800s. On its republication in 2004, the *New York Review of Books* said the book "crackles with the jibes and jokes of generations while presenting a striking picture of a vagabond nation in perpetual self-pursuit." Rourke's contemporary, the critic Lewis Mumford, called *American Humor* "the most original piece of investigation and inter-pretation that has appeared in American cultural history. It is in every way a brilliant book." The praise is all the more remarkable given a time in which female scholars were often treated patronizingly by their male colleagues and critics.

In an introduction to the 2004 edition of *American Humor*, rock-and-roll critic Greil Marcus said Rourke sought to define the American "as a tall-tale teller, a fabulist spinning a yarn." Her three archetypes illustrate the thesis. The Yankee is a practical joker, going from town to town as a con man, winning his audiences and customers over with sheer bravura. The backwoodsman is a rough-hewn near-savage given to tall tales, such as Davy Crockett's story of wrestling a bear. The actor in blackface borrowed heavily, if not thieving outright, from a people whom a 1795 traveler of the South called "the great humorists of the nation." Summarizing the thesis of her work and, by implication, all of her criticism, Rourke wrote, "The Yankee seemed an aboriginal character sprung suddenly, long-sided and nimble, from the gray rocks of his native soil. Surely he was no simple son of the Pilgrim fathers."

American Humor cemented Rourke's place as a leading American cultural critic. It also propelled her into a productive decade in which she authored biographies of backwoodsman Davy Crockett, naturalist John James Audubon, and painter and photographer Charles Sheeler.

The first two subjects were natural for Rourke. Both men had long since stridden into the annals of American myth. *Davy Crockett*, a 1935 Newbery honor book, also bolstered Rourke's finances; she sold the book's film rights, although the movie was never made.

Audubon fascinated Rourke for several reasons, perhaps the least of which were the results of his work as a student and painter of wildlife. Audubon was a man of myth who, arriving on American shores in 1803, was rumored to be the lost Dauphin of France, spirited away from the guillotine and adopted out. Rourke sought to debunk the notion that Audubon was a naive student of nature, wandering through the forest primeval. Rather, he was a sharp observer of people as well as nature, robust with pioneer spirit. And like many an ambitious American, he took great risks in pursuit of his dream, nearly bankrupting his family to publish *The Birds of America*.

Reviewer R. L. Duffus of the *New York Times* was impressed. "No summarizing review can do justice to Miss Rourke's treatment of the subject—all one can say is that she has succeeded somehow in looking at Audubon's life in somewhat the same way he looked at a bird. She has made a biography which is the best possible introduction to Audubon for a modern reader," Duffus wrote.

Rourke did some of her writing in North Muskegon, overlooking Bear Lake. A visitor in 1933 described this writing den as "a delightfully low, rambling house."

Although Rourke's success brought her into the company of talents such as Edmund Wilson, Malcolm Cowley, and William Carlos Williams, Rourke shunned the limelight, preferring the quiet, focused life of research, writing, and the hearth she shared with her mother. She may, too, have returned to Grand Rapids after forays to the East because of a distaste for the shine and sound of the literary world. Writing her mother from the MacDowell Colony in New Hampshire, an artists' retreat where she hobnobbed with the likes of Thornton Wilder, she said, "As usual after doing outside things rather steadily with people in the late afternoons and evenings I'm fed up and want to be alone." Grand Rapids, by contrast, had a Midwestern tranquility where she could mete out time for friends and other social demands as she chose.

But there were hidden depths. When Rourke discussed the American character, "she described it in terms of fantasy and emotion, and . . . she spent her career in an effort to establish a national identity," a biographer observed. This is particularly striking in light of her self-characterization as a "mystic." "And added to that," she wrote, "there is something wild in me." This energy fueled her work.

During the 1930s, she took on projects that dovetailed with her scholarly interests. She organized a National Folk Festival in St. Louis in 1934, and in 1936 became editor of the Index of American Design, part of the New Deal's Federal Art Project. In that role she oversaw the compilation of representative American folk forms, a job that enabled her to further her study of Americana.

Rourke spent years working on her magnum opus, a stunningly ambitious history of American culture. Conceived in the mid-1930s, it was to be a multivolume chronicle. She collected thousands of small blue slips of paper recording information on a multitude of items of American culture. She planned a two hundred thousand–word book cataloging and discussing regional development of music, graphic arts, literature, and crafts. Fellow critics awaited the massive work as a major advance in American letters.

Fate thwarted her plans. In March 1941 she slipped on the icy front porch of her Grand Rapids home and broke a vertebra. Apparently unwilling to trouble her mother, she crawled into the house. Only in the morning did she summon help. After several days in the hospital, as she prepared to go home, an embolism took her life.

Lamenting her death, John Chamberlain of the *New York Times* said her passing "went largely unnoticed, yet it was one of the most unfortunate calamities that could have befallen American criticism . . . Miss Rourke was always at great pains to show how American air, American landscape and American conditions subtly altered both the scale and the texture of our cultural inheritances from the Old World. More than anyone else, she has provided us with a real sense of our cultural origins."

Rourke's voice wasn't stilled at death. Her friend, the critic Van Wyck Brooks, sifted through her incomplete final project and published it as *The Roots of American Culture* in 1942. Far shorter than the ambitious panorama Rourke had envisioned, it was this work that the *Times*'s Chamberlain celebrated, even while mourning the loss of the complete project, and the loss of Constance Rourke herself. Others carry on work in her name: the American Studies Association annually awards the Constance M. Rourke prize for the best article published in the *American Quarterly* journal.

Inducted into the Michigan Women's Hall of Fame in 2004, Rourke is buried near a marker in Grand Rapids's Woodlawn Cemetery that links her to her mother in death as in life. Both names appear on the marker. Underneath the daughter's is this simple declaration: "American Biographer. Art Critic. Authority on Folklore." Like Rourke, it is no-nonsense—and puts America first.

Works

Trumpets of Jubilee (New York: Harcourt, Brace & Co., 1927).

Troupers on the Gold Coast, or The Rise of Lotta Crabtree (New York: Harcourt, Brace & Co., 1928).

American Humor: A Study of the National Character, reprint (1931; New York: New York Review Books Classics, 2004).

Davy Crockett (New York: Harcourt, Brace & Co., 1934).

Audubon (New York: Harcourt, Brace & Co., 1936).

Charles Sheeler: Artist in the American Tradition (New York: Harcourt, Brace & Co., 1938).

The Roots of American Culture, ed. Van Wyck Brooks (New York: Harcourt, Brace & World, 1942).

Sites

Grave: Woodlawn Cemetery, Grand Rapids, Block 5, Lot 347, Grave 4

Michigan Women's Historical Center and Hall of Fame, 213 W. Malcolm X Street, Lansing

Allan John Braitwaite Seager

The Forgotten Hemingway

February 5, 1906–May 10, 1968
Born and lived most of his life in Michigan

· ·

The best stories outlive their authors. Usually, however, the author's name remains attached. Not so with Allan Seager of Michigan. One of his stories is so striking that it has been borrowed, imitated, transmuted, and plagiarized dozens of times without attribution. It is typical of a man dubbed "one of the greatest American writers ever to be forgotten." Seager and the rest of his work deserve better.

Born in Adrian in February 1906, Allan John Braitwaite Seager experienced a childhood largely free of the drama that would characterize his early adulthood. His father was often on the road, leaving his mother Emma as a predominant influence. Reading to the young boy and his sister, she incubated his early interest in books. She also patiently answered his incessant questions and encouraged him to read any book in the house.

A renowned salesman for the Peerless Wire and Fence Company, Arch Seager contributed to his son's future career by returning home with compelling stories of the people and places he had visited. Allan acquired another writer's tool—the power of observation—watching mill workers coming and going past the family home every weekday. His native intelligence was another asset. In the middle of first grade, he was promoted to second.

Adolescence was more complicated. When Arch's employer transferred him to Memphis, Tennessee, the family went with him. The eleven-year-old Allan was furious at being uprooted. He angrily promised never to speak to his schoolmates and nearly kept the pledge for the first year. His concerned parents enrolled him in athletics at the local YMCA, where he became a talented swimmer. His prowess in the pool resulted in victories in local competitions, won him acclaim, and melted his reserve. He began to open up and was glad to be accepted.

In his autobiographical "memoir as fiction" *A Frieze of Girls*, Seager offers a few glimpses of family time from his teens—as a fifteen-year-old having a rare conversation with his aging grandfather about the latter's experience on the Gettysburg battlefield, and as the innocent who is shocked when his uncle suggests the now-deceased old man was difficult and will not be much missed.

Seager yields up a little more of his youth in "Under the Big Magnolia Tree," a chapter in *A Frieze of Girls*. Smitten in his sophomore year of high school by the sight of a lovely girl, he decides to impress her by trying out for the high-school football team. He gets his big chance when the first-string center withers in the southern heat in a game against a team from Tunica, Mississippi. Seager faces the giant defensive center. The big country boy has no moves other than falling on Seager. Seager outwits him by jumping back as soon as he snaps the ball. He makes "a couple of fancy tackles from behind," but the girl he craves is unimpressed.

Finding out that she is eighteen to his sixteen, Seager almost gives up. But he is undaunted, pursuing Helen ardently, if awkwardly. He spots "the most beautiful roses I had ever seen" at a flower stand, buys a dozen for fifty cents, has them wrapped in a newspaper, and takes them to his beloved. Arriving at her apartment, he presents the wrapped bouquet; when she unwraps them, there are no roses, only stamens. The petals have fallen off. Seager now knows why he got a bargain. "I dropped the whole mess on the floor and ran."

The romance is ill-fated. In his last glimpse of her, she is walking off with a "long tall rawboned ugly guy" probably ten years his senior, who can provide the material life Helen desires. And Allan is off to a different fate.

In 1925 his mother died of cancer, suffering uncomplainingly. As Seager left her room one day, she smiled and winked at him from her bed. A few hours later, she was dead. Her grace in the shadow of death left a deep impression of dignity that he would emulate as adversity struck him.

Michigan remained home in Seager's heart, and in the fall of 1925 he returned to the state and enrolled at the University of Michigan. Confident

Seager's happiness at his Victorian House in Tecumseh was a sharp contrast to his lacerating criticism of mid-twentieth century American society, expressed in novels like *Amos Berry*.

in his intellect (and a little smug), he was cynical about his admission to the school: "The entrance requirements are so low," he wrote in his diary, "that I wonder their halls are not filled with chattering morons. They probably are."

Seager excelled in his studies and in the pool, becoming an All-American swimmer. He maintained a private reserve in the midst of his campus popularity as a star athlete. A biographer notes, "He gave the appearance of belonging, and he did belong, but at the same time he followed his own dictates. He studied individuals functioning in groups; he learned not only from classes and reading but from observation."

Seager traveled to Oxford in the fall of 1930 as a Rhodes Scholar. He initially found himself at home among English classmates who, like Seager, concealed their passions behind a cool façade. Later he looked behind the mask, finding more similarities than differences between his American and English classmates—all interested in education as a means to the ends of income, position, and security rather than a pursuit for its own sake.

Seager was excelling in his Oxford studies and athleticism, swimming and rowing, when in the winter of 1932 he was diagnosed with tuberculosis. Forced to withdraw, he was treated at the Trudeau Sanitarium in Saranac Lake, New York. After nearly a year, he was discharged in good health. Life in the sanitarium provided him with material for fiction and awareness of his mortality, fueling his commitment to writing.

Successfully applying for a third year at Oxford, Seager had four months on his hands before resuming schoolwork. He found an inexpensive lodging and devoted himself to writing. The result was a remarkable first story.

Published first in the *London Mercury* and later revised and placed in an American setting in a collection of Seager's short stories, "The Street" resonated so well with readers that it went on to become legendary, rewritten and remade without attribution, published in magazines and broadcast on radio and television. Visiting Brazil, Seager recognized his plagiarized story in a Portuguese-language magazine while browsing in a doctor's waiting room. Seager told a British journalist, "I would gladly sell the rights to it for a hundred dollars, as it makes me so mad every time someone pinches it."

The story takes place in a hospital room, which two patients share. One is beside the only window and describes in detail the events daily unfolding on the street outside. "Every day Whitaker gave him something new, a dogfight, the new milk wagon, or a householder smoking in his back yard. These bright fragments he inserted carefully into the whole and trimmed and polished until the wall before him almost became a window through which he too could see the street."

The listening patient is increasingly envious of his roommate's privileged position—so much so, that when the roommate suffers a seizure, he lets him die rather than summoning the nurse. Inheriting the dead man's bed, the survivor looks out the window to see only a perpetually empty courtyard. His roommate's stories had been fashioned from imagination.

In the plagiarized versions, the patient's act of omission does not always appear. Instead, the emphasis is on the wonder of the human mind finding solace in dire circumstances and helping others. Summarizing an altered version of the story, an anonymous commentator on a website devoted to debunking urban legends draws this lesson: "There is tremendous happiness in making others happy, despite our own situations." Seager's more mordant approach takes a darker view of human nature. The tale derives from experience—but not literally. "I was in a TB hospital," he said. "I was the guy without the window. The only difference was that I always pressed the button."

"The Street" won Seager notice, leading to literary fame of a kind when his second story, "This Town and Salamanca," was published in 1934. The story features John Baldwin, who travels far and wide from his small Midwestern town. His friends, never venturing far from the community, keenly await his return each time and ask him to tell of his experiences, which provide them with vicarious happiness. Finally, Baldwin returns permanently to town. He fattens up, becomes a banker, and settles in the crowd, his youth now spent—and forcing his former listeners to face the fact that their dreams have crumbled, and their youth is also over.

The early stories generated impressive comparisons. Dedicating the 1935 edition of *Best American Short Stories* to Seager, series editor E. J. O'Brien said that the "apostolic succession of the American short story" ran from Sherwood Anderson to Ernest Hemingway to Allan Seager.

This success opened the door to prolific magazine writing. Over the decades, he published approximately eighty short stories and dozens of articles for everything from *Esquire* and *Good Housekeeping* to *Sports Illustrated*.

Seager also parlayed the notoriety of "The Street" and "The Town and Salamanca" into an assistant editorship at *Vanity Fair* in New York City. In a year and a half, he authored thirteen stories for the magazine and met celebrities—including Katharine Hepburn, Walt Disney, and Cole Porter—but reported himself "blasé" about the famous.

In the autumn of 1935 he returned to Ann Arbor. He would spend nearly all of his remaining years as a faculty member at the University of Michigan. To those who wondered why he gave up the glamour of New York City for the Midwest, Seager replied that he felt at home in Michigan.

Seager purchased a farm in Onsted, not far northwest of Adrian, and in fall 1939 moved there to attend to his ailing father. In November he married Barbara Watson. When war broke out in 1941, Seager volunteered but was turned down, in part because of his previous bout of tuberculosis. Meanwhile, he worked on his first novel. Published in 1943, *Equinox* briefly became a bestseller before a wartime paper shortage halted printing. *Equinox* was widely and mostly favorably reviewed—unlike his subsequent novels.

One of Seager's few forays from Michigan during the last half of his life was a year spent teaching at Bennington College in 1944–45. Urged on by friend Theodore Roethke, already on the Bennington faculty, Seager closely observed the great poet, gathering insights that would serve him as Roethke's biographer.

Returning to Michigan in 1945, Seager bought a Victorian house in Tecumseh, a shorter drive from Ann Arbor than Onsted. It became his residence for the rest of his life. Seager, Barbara, and daughters Mary (born in 1943) and Laura (born in 1948) were now happily together. The same year Laura was born, Seager's second novel, *The Inheritance*, appeared. But these milestones were overshadowed by Barbara's diagnosis of multiple sclerosis. Much of Seager's energy was invested in her care until her death in 1966. Tending to her was his duty, he believed; he resisted placing his wife in a nursing home until he no longer had the capacity to care for her.

Despite his added burdens, Seager remained committed to his work as a teacher and writer. In 1950, he published a collection of his stories, *The Old Man of the Mountain*. Oliver Prescott of the *New York Times* said Seager "writes smoothly and adroitly, with a sharp focus on character, and a nice gift for satire and irony," adding that the author was an "even better writer of short stories than he is a novelist."

Seager's most ambitious novel, *Amos Berry*, was published in 1953. Often employing a Hemingwayesque staccato cadence, the book advances the theme of most of Seager's later work: the twentieth-century American man crushed under the weight of organization and specialization, falling out of touch with the verities that sustained the nation and its people in America's early days.

Amos Berry is a successful businessman in a southeast Michigan town. Something is missing from his work, marriage, and life; increasingly aware of his emptiness, Amos becomes obsessed with murdering his boss, Walt Rickert. It's nothing personal. Although Rickert has a pinched, selfish character, he is reasonably good to Amos. Rather, Amos sees his act as a blow against the monotonous comforts and customs of American life—and against the indignity of work void of meaning, merely part of an organized economy. Told through the eyes of his ultimately forgiving son Charles, the novel is a meditation on the decline of American spirit under the weight of modernization, and the chance for renewal by returning to labor and life with meaning. A competitor buys out Amos's company, and he uses his payout to buy and work a farm. Did Amos's rebellion make a difference? Not long before story's end, Charles observes, "You were shooting at a system and all you killed was a man." His father replies, "That's right. All I killed was a man." A new generation will have to reform that system.

The novel did not do well commercially, and critics either misread or did not appreciate its subtleties. Prescott of the *Times* wrote, "Although *Amos Berry* is a serious and skillful book, continuously interesting, it yet fails to be successful as a work of fiction. One never quite believes in Amos's crime."

Although crushed by the critical reception, Seager continued producing novels, including *Hilda Manning* in 1956 and *Death of Anger* in 1960. Neither was a success. The publisher of *Death of Anger*—McDowell, Obolensky— became bankrupt just as the novel came off the presses, robbing Seager of attention for what would prove to be his last novel.

More satisfying was acclaim for his translation of Stendhal, accepted for publication on the twenty-first submission. *Memoirs of a Tourist* expressed his love for France, which he had visited while at Oxford and again in 1956, and for one of his favorite authors.

Seager's last two books were nonfiction. *A Frieze of Girls*, published in 1964, was a surprise hit. A collection of stories Seager had published in magazines, the wryly humorous, sometimes self-deprecating material cannot be taken as factual autobiography, although it touches on his life from adolescence and early adulthood. Seager's view was that each of us creates a narrative of our lives that, coupling memory and wish, is as much fiction as nonfiction. The title derives from an answer he gave to a friend's question about what stood out when he thought back to age twenty. "It was a kind of frieze of girls and long aimless car rides at night," said Seager. In an introduction to a 2004 reissue of the book, writer Charles Baxter described his reaction to the stories: "I almost fell out of my chair in surprise and happiness."

His final work appeared after his death in 1968. *The Glass House*, his biography of Michigan-born Theodore Roethke, is regarded by some critics as his best work. With keen insight into his late friend's mercurial character, Seager illuminates the poet's majesty and madness, building a case for Roethke's place in the American literary canon. Yet the book came at a price. In the midst of the writing, Seager became ill with lung cancer, and spent much of his flagging energy fighting and then yielding to excisions insisted on by Roethke's widow. Although admitting he was sacrificing quality, Seager was anxious for publication of the book while he lived. But when he died in May 1968, *The Glass House* was several months from rolling off the presses. It won great praise despite the compromised text. Critic Hugh Kenner declared it "the best American biography."

Several critics noted the parallels between the two men and suggested that Seager was writing almost as much about himself as about Roethke. A *New Republic* reviewer said that Seager had "an undeniable identification with a great many features of Roethke's life." Stephen E. Connelly added, "One could proceed slowly through the whole book, pulling sentence after sentence from each page, showing that the descriptions of Roethke are quite often also descriptions of Seager." The consensus was that this deepened rather than detracted from the work.

Seager's love of Michigan comes through in his use of it—particularly his home ground of Lenawee County—as a backdrop in his last four novels and much of his nonfiction. Upon returning to Michigan in 1935, he said in praise, "I was over home [Adrian] the other day. The country cries out for someone like Breughel to do it." In *The Glass House*, Seager said in an aside, "No one has ever made anything of the light of Michigan—it deserves as much attention as the sun of Andalusia."

After Seager's death, Sheridan Baker, editor of the *Michigan Quarterly Review*, commented, "His best stories are those that, like Hemingway's, are really autobiographical meditations, some somber, some wonderfully comic, as the mind recalls the smudge and shine, the stench and fragrance, of former times, shaping them a bit toward some fictional point, forming them again around some shaded remembrance or projection of one's former self."

Seager's writing is compulsively readable and, even when polemical, entertaining as well as provocative. Typically classified as a minor writer, Seager explored major themes, and at times succeeded in translating his concerns into high art.

Works

NOVELS
Equinox (New York: Simon and Schuster, 1943).
The Inheritance (New York: Simon and Schuster, 1948).
Amos Berry (New York: Simon and Schuster, 1953).
Hilda Manning (New York: Simon and Schuster, 1956).
Death of Anger (New York: McDowell, Obolensky, 1960).

SHORT STORY COLLECTIONS
The Old Man of the Mountain (New York: Simon and Schuster, 1950).
A Frieze of Girls: Memoirs as Fiction (New York: McGraw-Hill, 1964; reissued, Ann Arbor: University of Michigan Press, 2004).

NONFICTION WORKS
They Worked for a Better World (New York: Macmillan, 1939).
The Glass House: The Life of Theodore Roethke (New York: McGraw-Hill, 1968).

TRANSLATION
Stendhal's *Mémoires d'un Touriste/Memoirs of a Tourist* (Evanston, IL: Northwestern University Press, 1962).

Sites

Home at 309 West Chicago Boulevard, Tecumseh
Main Street in Adrian

Glendon Swarthout

Impossible to Pin Down

April 8, 1918–September 23, 1992
Born near Pinckney, obtained degrees at the University of Michigan and Michigan State University
and taught at both

The signature work of most popular authors corresponds to a genre—biography, history, detective novel, romance. Those who craft cowboy sagas rarely stray beyond arid prairies and craggy buttes. Despite scoring his biggest successes with Westerns, Glendon Swarthout resisted categorization. He even made famous—and infamous—a ritual of modern American youth.

Home in Swarthout's early life was the countryside near Pinckney and then the small city of Lowell. In an autobiographical sketch, Swarthout remembered his childhood, a little tongue-in-cheek, as unremarkable.

> I tipped over a high chair and broke my nose. I required the average number of diapers. World War I ended. At age four I suggested to a friend that we steal a loaf of warm bread from the bakery wagon that peddled our street, and eat the entire loaf. This we did. We had bellyaches of epic proportions, we learned a lesson, and I lost a friend because his parents told him that if he ever played with me again I would kill him, and if I didn't, they would.

A successful student in all but math, he was a scrawny high-school string bean, dropped from the football team after a week, weighing ninety-nine pounds. Books and music were his playing fields. His talent on the accordion led to engagements with dance orchestras, which provided a modest income and, like many of his experiences, fodder for later fiction. Between his junior and senior years, he played with Jerry Schroeder and the Michigan State College Orchestra at a Charlevoix resort for ten dollars a week.

When Swarthout was fourteen, his grandfather brought out of storage a Colt revolver and cavalry saber, carried by Glendon's great-grandfather during service in the 10th Michigan Cavalry in the Civil War. The weaponry touched off his imagination. As the oldest son, Glendon was allowed to choose between the two weapons when he turned twenty-one. He chose the revolver and kept it on the wall over his desk ever after. Late in life, he wrote that the weapons "enlisted me in the 10th Michigan Cavalry. For a seven-year hitch, I rode every road in the south, galloping, galloping. I yelled and waved that saber and skewered the foe by regiment. I hauled out that Colt and mowed 'em down, and U. S. Grant himself patted me on the back."

Two other experiences of youth cultivated the artist's imagination. He attended almost every Saturday's movie, often a "hell-for-leather Western." Once, his parents took him to see a live program celebrating the Old West, which included Native Americans performing dances. Swarthout was spellbound by the costumes, chants, and drumming.

For three summers during his undergraduate college career, he was the lead singer for a four-member band that played at the Pantlind Hotel in Grand Rapids. The quartet played five nights a week, the future author reaping a handsome sixty dollars weekly and his own room at the hotel. Majoring in English, Swarthout acquired a bachelor of arts degree from the University of Michigan in 1939.

He initially put his writing ability to work churning out advertising copy in support of Cadillac motor vehicles and Dow Chemical Company for a Detroit firm, Macmanus, John and Adams, housed in the Fisher Building. He married Kathryn Vaughn, whom he had known since the age of twelve and wooed as an undergraduate, on December 28, 1940. Not long after, he quit the copywriting life and became a traveling correspondent, wandering with Kathryn across South America and dispatching tales of their

Glendon Swarthout's panoramic sweep of storytelling is illustrated by two of the successful films made from his novels, *Where the Boys Are* and *The Shootist*. Courtesy of Miles Hood Swarthout, used with permission. All rights reserved.

adventures to twenty-two small newspapers back in the States for $212.50 a month.

While anchored in Barbados in December 1941, the couple learned of the attack on Pearl Harbor and immediately decided to return home. It wasn't easy. A series of short hops across the sea was necessary to avoid patrolling U-boats. The Swarthouts' sister ship was torpedoed. The journey to New York City took five months.

Too light at 117 pounds to qualify for Officer Candidate School, Swarthout joined his wife on the assembly line at an auto factory converted to bomber production at Willow Run—two words that would become the title of his first published novel in 1943. A commercial and artistic clunker, the now hard-to-find *Willow Run* was written off by Swarthout as his "training novel." The *Saturday Review* declared, "The factory scenes and processes, while they are so styled and staccato that they are sometimes exceedingly confusing, are much more interesting than the drama . . . The story, slight enough, is undeveloped even as a slight story. The author seems to be more interested in the plant and the plane, as the reader is very likely to be."

Swarthout beefed up and enlisted in the army in 1943. Anticipating intense combat in what would become the battle of Anzio, Italy, Swarthout was instead pulled from the front after seventeen hours by headquarters, which needed a writer to record incidents and heroes in the coming campaign to qualify recipients for the Congressional Medal of Honor, Silver Star, and other commendations—the "largest piece of luck" in his life to that time besides meeting Kathryn, he observed.

Swarthout did see six days of combat, landing with the infantry at St. Tropez, collecting eyewitness testimony to support often posthumous medals. The assignment—and meditations on the nature of courage—would become part of the story line in his novel *They Came to Cordura*. Reflecting on his wartime experience, he said once, "I met and came to know heroes. I wrote about incredible deeds on the battlefield. I came to believe profoundly that heroism lies latent in all of us, and all we need to evoke it is the right circumstances."

In late September 1944, just before his unit was to participate in the invasion of Germany, Swarthout ruptured a disc in his spine while unloading a truck, an injury never addressed by surgery. The resulting pain would dog him the rest of his life. He was sent home, discharged at the rank of sergeant.

Swarthout went back to school, obtaining a master's degree from the University of Michigan in 1946 and winning the Hopwood Award for a novel. Son Miles was born on May 1 of the same year. Swarthout taught freshman English at the university, finding he liked it, but "ended many a class wet with sweat" because the students were so bright. After teaching for two years at the University of Maryland, Swarthout took the family to Mexico and wrote for six months. Reviewing the manuscript, he decided it was lousy, "burned the manuscript for hot water for a shower, took that shower, packed us up, and it was Gringoland again."

In the fall of 1951, Swarthout began teaching at what was then Michigan State College. He received a doctorate in literature from MSC in 1955. He began to sell short stories to magazines, including *Cosmopolitan*, the *Saturday Evening Post*, and *Esquire*. He had found his professional path: he would teach college students and write fiction on the side.

Swarthout sold a story, 1954's "A Horse for Mrs. Custer," to Columbia Pictures for $2,000. It was good enough to become a film, *Seventh Cavalry*, starring Randolph Scott. It was a better story than movie. The story's haunting evocation of the aftermath of the Battle of the Little Bighorn puts it several notches above standard Western fare.

Swarthout was on the brink of fame. In 1958, *They Came to Cordura* deservedly became a bestseller. An anti-Western of sorts, the novel features a protagonist, Major Thorn, who is tainted by an episode of cowardice under fire in the 1916 American hunt for Mexican revolutionary Francisco "Pancho" Villa and his men. Ironically, Thorn is tasked with chronicling episodes of bravery to be used as documentation for the Congressional Medal of Honor. He plunges deeply into the assignment, trying to discern the nature of courage.

The novel becomes an epic journey as Thorn is ordered to protect five Medal of Honor candidates by detaching them from combat and making for the town of Cordura. Along the way, the unit is unexpectedly assaulted by raiders and faces daunting heat and thirst. Thorn capably, if not without some errors of judgment, leads the men and a captive woman toward their destination. At camp one night, he raves to his charges, "For a few minutes you proved that there is something above and beyond the law of nature, that the human race is human after all. In the space of those few minutes you became great men." But in truth they are only men. When Thorn's cowardice is revealed to the group by one of them, he faces their menacing contempt. The line between hero and coward blurs. Yet even in degradation Thorn finds transcendence. The *Chicago Tribune* called the book "a strong, harsh, haunting novel which will outlast most of the season's fiction . . . An ironic and revealing study of courage and cowardice."

Again, Hollywood lapped up Swarthout's story. *Cordura* became a vehicle for Gary Cooper. For the only time in his career, Swarthout worked on the screenplay of his novel. He netted a handsome $250,000 from Columbia Pictures for rights to the story. At age thirty-nine, Swarthout had won his independence to write for a living.

The author's next literary adventure put him on a plane to Florida. Listening to his Michigan State students excitedly discuss their plans for beach time during spring break in 1958, Swarthout decided to do field research in Fort Lauderdale. The result was *Where the Boys Are*, a chronicle of riotous young people drinking, playing, romancing, and talking deep into the night as they thaw out from the northern winter. Swarthout originally entitled the book *Unholy Spring*, but was persuaded to take a cue from a female college student who, when asked by a reporter for *Time* magazine why she would go to Florida for spring break, replied, "That's where the boys are."

The novel is credited with turning a Florida spring break from a lark for a relative few into a rite for a few million. Although most young people came to Florida for simple escape, the exuberance of some exceeded legal limits. The sheriff of Bay County, Florida, containing the Panama City beach, established a spring-break jail at the beach in 2012, eliminating the need to haul overintoxicated or otherwise misbehaving revelers twenty-five miles to the conventional jail. "You're talking about two million people coming through our area in a 47-day period. And they did not come to go to church," the sheriff said.

Narrating the novel in breathy first-person is undergraduate Merritt, who describes herself as five-foot-nine and 37–28–38. She explains why so many young people take their spring break in Fort Lauderdale:

"Why do they come to Florida? Physically to get a tan . . . Also, they are pooped. Many have mono . . . Psychologically, to get away . . . and besides, what else is there to do except go home [for spring break] and further foul up the parent-child relationship? Biologically, they come to Florida to check the talent." The novel proceeds in this tone, with plenty of drinking and necking.

While the 1960 film made from *Where the Boys Are* (starring Connie Francis and George Hamilton) is remembered for celebrating the light-hearted escapism of spring break, it and the book also contain a somber undercurrent. Merritt suffers an unexpected consequence of the party life, and finds herself alone.

Swarthout was now a major novelist. In 1959 he left MSU for a position at Arizona State University, where he continued to teach English. He retired after four years there, devoting himself full-time to writing.

A novel that demonstrated his reach was *Bless the Beasts and Children*, published in 1970. Although set in Arizona, it is a Western in geography only. A group of six troubled adolescents are housed at a boys' camp that promises, "Send Us a Boy—We'll Send You a Cowboy!" But these kids are outcasts, one a bed-wetter, all of them unable for one reason or another to win the acceptance of the popular boys.

They are also far more sensitive than most of their peers. Witnessing the slaughter of buffalo in a planned "harvest" designed to cull the herd, the boys are sickened. They launch a desperate mission to rescue the noble beasts. On the way, they learn what it is to be a man—and that the going is difficult, even dangerous. Courage is again a Swarthout theme. It resonated, resulting in sales of more than 2 million.

Swarthout wrote fourteen published short stories. One is "Four Older Men," a sardonic takedown of romance. Looking down on a beautiful young woman and an adoring suitor in a bar in Washington, D.C., who are about to consummate their affair, the omniscient narrator watches them go their separate ways after just five pages. The words of author Thomas Wolfe, whose gravesite the woman had visited on an earlier, memorable date, play a big role in the split.

One of Swarthout's Westerns, 1975's *The Shootist*, left a deep imprint on American culture. The tale of a dying gunslinger come to town for his final weeks is written in spare prose. Reminiscing about his career without sentiment, the gunman decides on one last showdown—unlike any in Western lore.

The parallel between the circumstances of the protagonist and the actor who played him, John Wayne, are remarkable. John Books is dying of cancer, the same disease that would claim Wayne less than three years after the film's release. In one of his final roles, Wayne won critical acclaim. Frank Rich said, "Wayne makes a terminally ill character seem transcendentally alive."

Swarthout had a writing partner—his wife Kathryn, a poet and longtime columnist for *Women's Day* magazine. They cowrote six novellas for young readers. The *New York Times Review of Books* included one of them, *The*

Button Boat, in the list of the year's twenty best books for children in 1969. Son Miles received a Writers Guild nomination for Best Adaptation for the screenplay of *The Shootist* in 1976.

The son underscored his father's versatility. "Glendon never repeated himself or wrote any sequels, although book editors were certainly after him for *Where the Girls Are*, and the producers of *The Shootist* were interested in a follow-up film," Miles wrote in a postscript to a collection of Swarthout's short stories. "Such professional eclecticism made it tough for the critics, as well as his readers, to follow the body of his work, let alone anticipate what might be coming from his typewriter next."

Despite his unpredictability, Swarthout was a dependable source of cinematic and television material. Over half of the sixteen novels he wrote and several of his short stories were optioned, sold, or eventually made into motion pictures or movies for television. He was twice nominated for the Pulitzer Prize for Fiction, received an O. Henry Short Story Prize nomination, and was given a gold medal by the National Academy of Arts and Letters.

A longtime smoker, Swarthout died of emphysema in 1992. He was inducted into the Western Writers Hall of Fame in 2008. In addition to the Swarthout Awards for young writers that he and his wife endowed at Arizona State University, his legacy is an example of hard-to-surpass versatility, and a curiosity about the inner workings of human beings that resulted in vivid, unforgettable characters.

Works

Willow Run (New York: Thomas Y. Crowell Co., 1943).
They Came to Cordura (New York: Random House, 1958).
Where the Boys Are (New York: Random House, 1960).
Welcome to Thebes (New York: Random House, 1962).
The Cadillac Cowboys (New York: Random House, 1964).
The Eagle and the Iron Cross (New York: New American Library, 1966).
Loveland (Garden City, NY: Doubleday, 1968).
Bless the Beasts and Children (Garden City, NY: Doubleday, 1970).

The Tin Lizzie Troop (Garden City, NY: Doubleday, 1972).

Luck and Pluck (Garden City, NY: Doubleday, 1973).

The Shootist (Garden City, NY: Doubleday, 1975).

A Christmas Gift (also known as *The Melodeon*) (New York: Doubleday, 1977).

Skeletons (Garden City, NY: Doubleday, 1979).

The Old Colts (New York: D.I. Fine, 1985).

The Homesman (New York: Weidenfeld and Nicolson, 1988).

Pinch Me, I Must Be Dreaming (New York: St. Martin's Press, 1994).

Easterns and Westerns (East Lansing: Michigan State University Press, 2001).

Sites

Willow Run Michigan Historical Marker, B-24 Bomber Plant, Kirk Profit Drive, Ypsilanti Township

Amway Grand Plaza Hotel, formerly the Pantlind Hotel

Harold Titus

Author on the Forestry Frontier

February 20, 1888–October 9, 1967
Born, lived, and did most of his writing from the Traverse City area

Some books have influence beyond their artistic value. Shrugged off or sneered at by critics, they sell well or make a timely case that reshapes public opinion. When Traverse City author Harold Titus published the novel *Timber* in 1922, his fiction was a thinly disguised plea for state public policies to scientifically reforest northern Michigan's cutover lands, which had been abandoned by the lumber industry after it had shaved off virtually every tree of marketable value. Never mind that the novel included a love story that enabled Hollywood to make a silent film of it, *Hearts Aflame*. The romance most significant in Titus's work was the romance of conservation—the dream of replenishing the northern Lower Peninsula and the Upper Peninsula with continually renewable trees providing beauty, recreation, and economic return. In the process, millions of acres of logged-over wastelands would become wealth-generating lands.

In *Timber*, John Taylor, son of the wealthy lumber baron Luke Taylor, woos the fiercely independent Helen Foraker, an apt name for a lover of

Harold Titus wrote a novel that galvanized public support for the reforestation of Michigan. He also served on the state Conservation Commission for two decades. Courtesy of Charles W. Siffert and Loraine Anderson.

forestry. The young woman explains to John a new way of managing forests that will produce sustained return over the long haul. "Foraker's Folly," the locals call the ten thousand–acre tract her father replanted, jeering at a crop that they believe will take a thousand years to replace the primeval forest. But Helen sees more clearly. She declares,

> Less than fifty years ago this land was stripped of its pine; today it is maturing another crop. The same could have been done with any other piece that grew good trees: Just keep the fire out and nature would have done much in time . . . To exist as a nation, we must have forests; to have forests all we need to do for a beginning is to give this worthless land a chance. We can speed up its work by helping—by keeping out fire, by planting trees, by good forest practice.

John's father, proud of his role in harvesting—or denuding—Michigan's landscape of its original forest resource, tries to put a stop to Helen's scheme, but she refuses. In the end even Luke comes to see the wisdom, the utilitarianism, and the beauty of her reforestation work.

The film *Hearts Aflame* was shown in Lansing during the 1922 legislative session. Its climax, a raging forest fire that nearly destroys the Foraker plantation, may have helped persuade the lawmakers to make their "first decently generous" forest firefighting appropriation, Titus said. The book was "the first novel of conservation anywhere," said the outdoor writer Ben East. "It appeared at a psychological time. Many thinking persons in Michigan and other sections of the country were feeling a growing discontent with the policies of letting cutover lands lie idle year after year, scourged by annual forest fires, or of trying to plant hopeless farm colonies on this poor land, fit only for the growing of timber crops. *Timber* crystallized that discomfort. It was hailed as the prophet of a new order." *Traverse City Record-Eagle* city editor Jay Smith said, "Harold Titus, through the medium of a bully tale, shows the way out" of the state's cutover land crisis.

The book's fame expanded well beyond Michigan. Pennsylvania governor Gifford Pinchot, the architect of Theodore Roosevelt's national forest policy, hailed it. The *London Times* made note of it as heralding a new approach to American conservation.

Titus was no one-note author, however. An active imagination and writing skill fostered a range of novels.

Born February 20, 1888, in Traverse City, Titus came of age at a time when the lumber industry was exhausting the valuable white pine and hardwood of the region, leaving behind waste wood, or slash, that frequently erupted into catastrophic fires ravaging thousands of acres and taking many lives, providing fodder for *Timber*. At the same time, leaders of a burgeoning reforestation movement in Washington, D.C., supported by President Theodore Roosevelt, and in Michigan, cheered on by Forestry Commission chair Charles Garfield, were beginning to win converts to the cause. None of this escaped Titus.

A high school football player, Titus worked as a reporter at the *Traverse City Evening Record* while still a student. He graduated from Traverse City High School and then attended the University of Michigan from 1907 to 1911, also reporting on sports and campus events for the *Detroit News*. He left college because of an attack of tuberculosis and became a *News* crime and courts reporter. He then moved to Colorado and worked with cowboys. He married Beth Benedict in 1914 and returned to his hometown, becoming a fruit grower.

Several of Titus's early novels, presumably based on his time in Colorado, were Westerns, including *Bruce of the Circle A*, published in 1918. The story has its charm, although it draws from a stockpile of Western tropes. When beautiful Ann Lytton travels from the East to track down her dissipated husband Ned in Arizona, she encounters the noble cowboy Bruce Bayard attending to her drunken mate. Ann and Bruce soon form a romantic attachment that cannot be consummated because of Ann's adherence to her wedding vows. Knowing he may be redeeming a man who will forever keep him from Ann, Bayard takes Ned into his home in an attempt at rehabilitation. But the inebriate is too far gone and vicious in his refusal to change. A tense shootout climaxes the book. The once-forbidden love between Ann and Bruce can be fully expressed.

Despite the predictable plot, the novel is worthwhile for its commentary on authentic versus conventional morals, for patches of keen characterization, for its fine description of the Western landscape, and for its opening:

> Daylight and the Prescott-Phoenix train were going from Yavapai. Fifty paces from the box of a station a woman stood alone beside the track, bag in hand, watching the three red lights of the observation platform dwindle to a ruby unit far down the clicking ribbons of steel. As she watched, she felt herself becoming lost in the spaciousness, the silence of an Arizona evening.
>
> Ann Lytton was a stranger in that strange land. Impressions pelted in upon her—the silhouetted range against the cerise flush of western sky; the valley sweeping outward in all other directions to lose itself in the creeping blue-grays of night; droning voices of men from the station; a sense of her own physical inconsequence; her loneliness . . . and as a background, the insistent vastness of the place.

The Last Straw (1920) contains a variant on this plot. Pampered Jane Hunter comes west to survey her uncle's ranch, left to her upon his death. Facing skepticism from the hired hands, she nonetheless decides to maintain ownership and supervise the ranch. At her side is the quiet, formidable ranch hand and later foreman Tom Beck, whose initial doubts of Jane's capacity to succeed in a man's world dissolve in the face of her toughness. Their bond is tested and briefly thwarted by her venal, rejected lover from the East and the daughter of a claim-staker who seeks to block the ranch's cattle from a scarce water supply. In the end, love—and a resolute and remade Jane Hunter—prevail.

These novels and another Western, *I Conquered* (1916), preceded the author's turn to conservation themes and *Timber*. An incident in 1918 is said to have awakened Titus's conservation conscience. Returning home from domestic service in World War I, he took an outing along the Manistee River and saw poachers and their dogs pursuing a deer. The breach of sporting ethics disturbed him, stiffening his resolve to champion sound natural-resource management.

His love of the outdoors as much as his belief in rational management of forests fueled *Timber*, Titus said. "I saw my trout streams going to pot because ransacking lumbermen and neglected forest fires were changing their character."

Hearts Aflame earned Titus $3,500 in film rights purchased by Louis B. Mayer Productions, but the author grumbled about distortions in the final screen product. Besides the film fashioned from *Timber*, Titus drew writing credits for four movies, including *Shod with Fire* (1920), based on *Bruce of the Circle A*.

Timber also earned Titus a reputation as a conservation leader, and consequently, Michigan governor Fred Green appointed him to the state Conservation Commission in 1927. Titus would spend the bulk of the next twenty-two years in the prestigious but nonpaying post, helping steer Michigan conservation policy. Named chair of the commission's forest-fire committee, Titus made his initial priority the buildup of a state forest-fire service. His mission was a success. Michigan grew one of the best forest fire-fighting units among all state governments. Titus was not a general giving orders from safety far behind the battle lines. He sometimes joined forest firefighters with a shovel and knapsack.

Titus was a steady writer, producing articles and short fiction for magazines like *Collier's*, *Liberty*, *Redbook*, and *Ladies' Home Journal*. Set in Michigan's north woods during fire season, a 1944 story published in *Liberty* is a tale of a young man's coming of age in the face of danger. "Kindness'll Kill" features Morty Nesson, a protégé of conservation officer Joe Bell. When a potentially catastrophic blaze menaces the forest, Morty initially turns away from the life-threatening risk of carving a cutoff line with his tractor. Then, when Bell takes the wheel and is close to death, Morty discovers inner strength, rescuing Bell and assisting him in heading off the fire. Morty summarizes the message of the wartime story for Joe from the hospital bed where he recuperates: "I've had it too soft. I'd got the habit of shying off when the going looked hard. Having you—well, disgusted was the kick in the pants I needed."

But at the center of his periodical writings was *Field and Stream*, for which he was longtime conservation editor. Titus frequently voiced his advanced conservation views through the character of the Old Warden, a churlish fish-and-game cop, outdoor observer, and prophet. Nationally known conservation sage Aldo Leopold called the Old Warden stories "a really remarkable attempt to translate wildlife ecology and management into the lay-jargon of sportsmen." In many of the stories, the Old Warden talks up the science behind conservation, challenging the prejudices of politicians and sportsmen alike.

In one departure from the norm, "The Old Warden Goes Highbrow," the curmudgeon muses with model outdoorsman Harvey Painter on the aesthetic values associated with time spent in search of fish and game. They agree on the good stream-restoration work of government agencies, but also agree that something has been missing. Says Painter: "It ain't quite in my line, talkin' about beauty. And maybe I'm breakin' up—gettin' old—when I fuss about some states that maybe are breakin' their necks to step up the fish-carryin' capacity of their waters and givin' no thought to the looks of the job." But the Old Warden agrees that stocking fish and game is only part of the job of conservation—restoring the appearance of woods and streams is also critical.

Meanwhile, Titus turned out more novels. *Black Feather* (1936) is anchored at Mackinac Island in the early 1800s, when the isle was a hub of the fur trade. The young protagonist, Rodney Shaw, wins his black feather—a sign of leadership—by successfully fighting a voyageur. Determined to make his living as a fur trader, he faces and surmounts numerous obstacles, including a false accusation of murder. Ultimately, he wins the love of a beautiful young woman. The *New York Herald Tribune* called it "crammed with action and good he-man stuff . . . historically faithful" to the lives and people of the Old Northwest.

The dual tracks of Titus's career—writing and activism—won him two notable honors. He received an honorary master of arts degree from the University of Michigan in 1934. In 1951, he was awarded the Wildlife Society's prestigious Leopold Medal for his work on behalf of conservation.

Through his writings and advocacy, Titus left an enduring legacy. Among his other conservation achievements, Titus is credited with helping found the Izaak Walton League, a leading fish, game, and habitat advocacy group. Closer to home, he is credited with being a cofounder of the National Cherry Festival and helping in the transfer of the Old Mission Peninsula lighthouse from federal to state and ultimately to township possession. The lighthouse and the waters through which it guided skippers at the tip of the peninsula are today a major tourist attraction.

During much of his life, Titus co-managed a fruit orchard on the Old Mission Peninsula containing approximately seven thousand cherry and apple trees. He lived in a house overlooking the west arm of Grand Traverse Bay.

When Titus left the Michigan Conservation Commission in 1949, a newspaper called him "Michigan's grand old man" of fish, game, and forest protection. Observers credited him with helping promote the recreation potential of the Upper Peninsula and building a popular constituency for conservation through his abundant writings. But those who appreciate Michigan's 3.9 million acres of state forestland—more than in any other state east of the Mississippi—can thank both his pen and his personal commitment.

In one of his final major published works, *The Land Nobody Wanted* (1945), Titus wrote, "It is not safe to say that Michigan's public domain, as we know now it, will remain so for all time. But of one thing we are reasonably certain: in the opinion of that segment of the public qualified to know, today's program for state acres is largely sound. That program has resulted from the blood, sweat and tears that earlier generations poured into the commonwealth's land problem."

That opinion is as fresh and accurate today as it was then.

Works

I Conquered (New York: A.L. Burt Co., 1916).

Bruce of the Circle A (Boston: Small, Maynard & Co., 1918).

The Last Straw (New York: A.L. Burt, 1920).

Timber (Boston: Small, Maynard & Co., 1922).

Beloved Pawn (New York: A.L. Burt, 1923).

Spindrift: A Novel of the Great Lakes (New York: Doubleday, Page, 1925).

Below Zero: A Romance of the North Woods (Philadelphia: Macrae Smith, 1932).

Code of the North (Philadelphia: Macrae Smith, 1933).

Flame in the Forest (Philadelphia: Macrae Smith, 1933).

Forest War (London: Skeffington and Son, 1934).

The Man from Yonder (New York: A.L. Burt, 1934).

Black Feather (Philadelphia: Macrae Smith, 1936).

The Land Nobody Wanted: The Story of Michigan's Public Domain (East Lansing: Michigan State College, Agricultural Experiment Station, Section of Conservation, 1945).

Sites

Michigan Historical Marker "Beginning of State Reforestation," Registered Site S0143, North Higgins Lake State Park, County Road 203, Higgins Lake

Oakwood Cemetery, Traverse City, Plat 2, Lot 137, Grave 4

Former Traverse City High School (now Central Grade School), 301 West Seventh Street, Traverse City

Orlando Bolivar Willcox

Heroic Author

April 16, 1823–May 11, 1907

Born and raised in Detroit; practiced law there before and after the Civil War, in which he famously represented Michigan

• •

Orlando Bolivar Willcox may have been the most indefatigable writer in Michigan history, producing a lifelong inventory of diaries, journals, letters, reports, and an autobiography that never quite made it into print. He was "possessed of marked literary tastes,"[1] having grown up with a father who loved books. He was an early contributor to the Whig Party organ the *Daily Advertiser*, and his first book featured irreplaceably colorful accounts of the frontier village of Detroit early in its American experience. And only in the 1990s was the true extent of his authorship discovered.

Named after South American military and political hero Simon Bolivar, Willcox also became one of the state's most notable servicemen. He was a West Point graduate, Mexican American and Seminole campaign veteran, and commander of Michigan's first volunteer Civil War regiment. He was wounded in its first major battle, captured, imprisoned for thirteen months, promoted to general, and honored for his bravery, including the Medal of

Orlando Bolivar Willcox was an early Detroiter, lawyer, soldier, Medal of Honor recipient, and lifelong writer. Courtesy of the Archives of Michigan.

Honor. He was one of Michigan's greatest military figures during four years of service from start to finish of America's bloodiest war. Virtually a career military man, he rejoined the postwar army to serve out west in the Indian conflicts, was honored when Arizona townspeople claimed his name as their community's, and capped his service by running the veterans' home in the nation's capital. Unfortunately for his legacy, he was no politician.

His early writings, though authored under a pseudonym, may have alienated a key supporter and cost him the opportunity for lasting fame. As he had spent most of his life away from home serving the nation, his name was largely forgotten back in Detroit. Neither the city nor his native state erected a monument to him, appropriated funds for a statue, hallowed the decades of his unselfish service. Although he helped save the nation, when it finally

Typical wood-framed house of 1840s' Detroit, the home of Ulysses S. Grant, Willcox's fellow West Point graduate and Mexican and Civil War hero, is shown here.

emerged in text a century later, his life story was entitled *Forgotten Valor*. This was accurate, but not at all fitting.

Orlando Bolivar Willcox was born in Detroit in 1823 when only 1,400 people lived there. Many were Native Americans; others were of French descent. His New England–born parents, Charles and Almira, immigrated to the almost wholly unsettled Michigan Territory shortly after the War of 1812. Charles became a successful hatter and furrier, one of five trustees of the town, and a lover of literature. He died prematurely of disease, leaving a widow and six children, Orlando not yet five years old. The community leaders came to the family's aid: Joseph Campau sold them property and Father Gabriel Richard ministered to them; *Detroit Free Press* founder Sheldon McKnight gave one son a job, Chancellor Elon Farnsworth another. Schoolmates included Friend Palmer, Sylvester Larned, and Alexander McKinstry. Orlando capitalized on a job as page for the territorial legislature, which met in the first Michigan Capitol at the head of Griswold Street, to pursue reading (doing so "assiduously," he remembered) and improve his writing. The youngster prepared a legislative manual for the fledgling government. One of the family homes was on the south side of Jefferson between Brush and Beaubien streets, where the Renaissance Center stands today.

When the time came to make his way in the world, Willcox's first thought was the ministry. It offered writing and speaking but little danger. He chose instead a military career, his first love. He journeyed to Washington, lobbied to go to West Point, labored for the support of the Michigan delegation—receiving it tepidly from the single member in the House of Representatives, Jacob M. Howard—and succeeded both with an appointment and a record to be proud of, graduating eighth in the class of 1847. The next decade found him in Mexico, Texas, Florida, and the western plains. He returned to civilian life in Detroit in 1857, taking up the practice of law with brother Eben. It bored him. He had written one book while in the army; now he tried to become a writer.

Willcox's first effort found a publisher in 1856. In the lighthearted *Shoepac Recollections: A Way-Side Glimpse of American Life*, he wrote of his "little antiquated city," where a traveler could be "quite certain of having passed the *ultima thule*,[2] when he would stumble with astonishment on our little community." Despite having "penetrated into regions where civilization grew dimmer and dimmer as he advanced," the visitor would find Detroit a pleasing place:

> He would see old-fashioned buildings, stores and dwellings forming a promiscuous row, with high gables and dormer-windows, roofs peaked like Vandyke hats, with their edges notched and painted red, and doors panelled into four parts, and opening by subdivisions, like modern window-shutters . . . One could not well imagine a pleasanter state of feeling than mutually existed, with sufficient distinction between the different castes or classes to prevent wrangling, and yet sufficient community of interest, prejudice, and pleasure to make everybody sociable.

Though a martial man, he could adopt a poet's perspective:

> In front of the house are the cherry-trees, and in the rear the pear and apple-orchards; and the traveller is surprised to find the best of fruit thus far beyond the pale of civilization—fruits brought from sunny France, and planted by the skillful Jesuit; apples, red to the core, large and luscious; cherry that rival nectarines; and pears of every variety, and of every season, from July to November. Nor will the patch of onions escape his notice: it is a Frenchman's flower-garden—the invariable concomitant of every family who may claim a foot square of mother earth. The fish-net or seine is stretched on the fence. The long, flint-lock duck gun, with leathern pouch and powder-horn, is hung on wooden hooks in the hall. The canoe is drawn up on the beach.

Shoepac was one of the earliest examples in the long tradition of writing about Michigan's lakes and streams. Take these lines on boatmen approaching the river post as "the sound of distant voices come stealing over the water":

> No music could be more lively or inspiring. It comes over the water—is accompanied by the splash of oars. It is roared out with the utmost spirit, too, by that most glorious of all instruments, the human voice. It has pealed through the woods, and over the river and lakes, for thousands of miles.

Shoepac[3] painted a bucolic setting, but the author unintentionally had made an enemy who would block promotion.

Willcox's next effort was a military romance. *Faca: An Army Memoir*[4] emerged from imagination, rather than his experience in Michigan. It spun a tale about Francisca, a young girl who "shall prove herself a woman, the man a child"—referring to the other main characters, Lieutenant Soldan, who had just graduated from the military academy, and William Marshal, who would win Faca's affection. Willcox found it appropriate to "wind up our story with a wedding, notwithstanding it grows fashionable to decry that sort of nonsense in a book." There were a few more flourishes, culminating in constructions like "Hark! the sweet music's coming from the Main! the harmony of Ocean's roundelay! How soft the mingled note!" After filling a volume with such fluff, Willcox next wrote a serialized story about West Point cadets that had a bit less fancifulness but a similar plot line. And then greater drama came.

Willcox endeavored to practice law earnestly after a literary career foundered, but his West Point training brought him more favorable attention. He served on the state's military board and called for better preparation should sectional conflict arise. Many regarded a war between Americans as unthinkable no matter their differences. On April 12, 1861, they were proved wrong when the U.S. installation named Fort Sumter in Charleston Harbor was fired upon by Southern secessionists. The Civil War had begun. On May 1, Willcox accepted a commission as colonel of the 1st Michigan Volunteer Infantry Regiment.

In Willcox's class at the military academy had been a number of future generals. On the Union side, his classmates included Ambrose Burnside,

John Gibbon, and Charles Griffin. A. P. Hill and Henry Heth fought for the South. Ahead of him had been George B. McClellan and "Stonewall" Jackson; afterward graduated John Buford and Robert Ransom. Only Willcox would have the honor of representing his class in receiving the Medal of Honor. It was bestowed in 1895 for his heroism at the first major battle of the war in the Eastern Theater, near Bull Run in Virginia. Leading his regiment of Michigan infantry on an incursion deeper into the Rebel lines than any other unit, he was wounded and captured.[5] After being exchanged, he returned to service for the rest of the war and ended it by leading the first units into the rail hub of Petersburg, raising the American flag over the city and precipitating the flight and surrender of Robert E. Lee that effectively ended the Confederacy. Michigan gave the Detroit native a hero's welcome. On the Fourth of July, 1866, he represented all Michigan troops by entrusting their battle-scarred regimental flags to the governor in an elaborate ceremony in Detroit's Campus Martius. The priceless collection remains on exhibit in the Michigan Historical Museum. His duties that day, however, were not nearly the end of his military service.

In July 1866 he received appointment as a regular army officer in command of the 29th U.S. Infantry Regiment, later in command of the 12th U.S. Infantry Regiment and commander of the Department of Arizona. The territorial legislature publicly thanked Willcox for his services, and a town founded as Maley's Camp was renamed for him. When the first train stopped in town with the department commander on board, townspeople recognized their benefactor and shouted "Willcox! Willcox! Willcox!" A reporter from Tucson wrote up the account in the *Arizona Daily Star* about the newly established habitation called Willcox.

The general—he had finally been awarded that rank—retired from the army in 1887, serving in a quasi-military role until 1892 as governor of the Soldiers' Home in Washington, D.C., where he resided. Summers found him in Canada to beat the heat; he passed away there in 1907, age eighty-five. Interment was in Arlington National Cemetery. It was a fitting honor, and the sizable monument over his grave, found in Section 1 of this hallowed ground, pays tribute to his patriotism.

Despite its seeming importance, that space is at the back of the cemetery away from most visitors, exemplifying treatment of Willcox during the war. Despite his bravery and leadership skills, he did not escape the political thickets that frequently made and broke Northern generals. He had no real patron; his antebellum Democrat identity cost him; and one politician undermined promotion. Jacob Howard, junior U.S. senator, was a stalwart Republican and anti-slavery advocate. Though not as bombastic as Zachariah Chandler, his Michigan senior in the chamber, Howard was no less zealous for the causes he championed. Willcox had lost him as a supporter thanks to *Shoepac*.

How could such a work, written under the "Major March" alias and purporting to be a trifling memoir, render Howard an antagonist? The answer lies in a character named O.H.P. Hustings, M.C. This Michigan politician proposed to send Mr. March to West Point—so far, so good—but there was a problem: Hustings was vainglorious. As a former politician at the state level, his election to Congress went to his head; he "seemed so delighted with his elevation, that like the clown in the farce, he stood ready to marry all the widows, and father all the children among his constituents."[6] That was not the only dig: the novel caustically referred to Hustings as a "virtuous politician" since the congressman advised unsuccessful candidates that they should have applied for a different opening. Instead, the "benevolent and disinterested statesman had appointed the sons of two political friends."[7] March had gone to West Point, but little thanks to the member of Congress.

Using the nom de plume enabled Willcox to poke fun at the deserving Howard. Or so he thought, for the author's identity evidently was no secret.[8]

Perhaps using a pen name enabled more than just satire, for the book dealt with some of the traumatic events of the author's life. Nothing is more compelling than the description of losing his father when a child, as the entire family—save one member—emerged from an influenza-like disease:

> After a while, one after another recovered, save one—the one, the all in all to my mother and me. I remember some person taking me silently by the hand one Sabbath morning. Every night on retiring to our room, my father was accustomed to come in gently . . . and kneel down on the floor at the bedside. This was likewise his custom on Sunday mornings. But during the last few weeks we had struggled through our prayers the best we could alone, and the burden of our petitions was for him. Our thoughts were full of this subject now, when one came to lead us

into his apartment. As soon as we reached the bedside we knelt down and clasped our little hands, ready for him to begin the supplication; but with a quick sob, the female who had brought us caught me in her arms, turned down the sheet which covered his face, and—

Oh God! was I, was I fatherless?[9]

Willcox overcame many obstacles, including the nearly lifelong absence of his father. He could not overcome the lack of a political patron or somehow win sufficient adulation from his fellow Michiganders. A statue of George A. Custer went up in Monroe in 1910; one on Belle Isle honoring Alpheus S. Williams was dedicated in 1921. The entry to the state capitol in Lansing is fronted by the 1898 statue of Governor Austin Blair; Campus Martius features the massive Soldiers and Sailors Monument, erected in 1867. Willcox knew of the latter two, for he survived military service long enough.

In 1999, nearly a century later, the many words that Willcox had penned came to light. A descendant had preserved them in her Washington, D.C., attic, and a writer of history from Michigan paid her a visit after hearing she had some of the general's papers. To his astonishment, he discovered a treasure trove of Willcox's lifetime of writing in an old wooden steamer trunk and several boxes. Instead of a contemplated biography, the historian decided to publish the author's original life story, since he had "told it so well himself."[10]

In a way, *Forgotten Valor* served as a fitting bookend to three other Michigan war memoirs. Immediately after the surrender in 1865, Sarah Emma Evelyn Edmonds published (by subscription)[11] a work combining autobiography with, in all likelihood, fantasy. *Nurse and Spy in the Union Army: Comprising the Adventures and Experiences of a Woman in Hospitals, Camps, and Battle-fields* told the story of Franklin Thompson—in reality, Ms. Edmonds, who disguised herself and served at (so she claimed, beyond) the front lines. No disguise was employed by the colonel commanding the Sixth Michigan Infantry, Edward Bacon of Niles, whose *Among the Cotton Thieves* was released in 1867.[12] John L. Ransom, quartermaster in the 9th Michigan Cavalry, spent months in Andersonville prison as a guest of the Confederacy. Returning to Jackson, he was mustered out of service on July 21, 1865, and went back to work as a reporter at the *Citizen*. At the urging of his editors, he published his prison diary in a series that ran in the newspaper for several months starting on October 17, 1865. His original diary, which filled three books, was lost in a fire, but the *Citizen's* series made its way to book form in 1881. When reprinted in 1963 it made the ranks of top sellers. These three war accounts were among the earliest in the Civil War library, certainly of the memoirs by participants. Willcox's is one of the last.

His accounts of war experiences remain riveting. While imprisoned after First Bull Run, he wrote of the day's combat from fresh recollection:

> The 1st Michigan . . . pushed on rapidly and regained my former position . . . My hope was now to turn the enemy's rear . . . We advanced to the point of woods, my men giving a loud cheer as I rode up to the right wing, and pushed to the rear of the enemy, now hotly engaged . . .
>
> We availed ourselves of a slight ravine, or gullet, and fought partly under cover. As soon as the enemy discovered our fire, their rear rank faced about with utmost coolness and began to return it, and it was during this sharp practice that my horse was shot in the front and lower part of the neck, and I was shot in the right fore arm . . . I saw men firing at me very deliberately, but I had passed through such hot work already that I had scarcely a faint idea of being hit, until suddenly I felt a severe shock, like that of electricity in my arm, which began to spin around like a top. This was followed by extreme faintness, such that it was with difficulty I could hold the rein in my left hand and guide the horse to the rear even a few steps . . .
>
> It must have been with great difficulty that the 1st Michigan cut their way back from their position, for the enemy were now on two sides of them, and I soon found were approaching on a third side . . . I discovered them and ordered the three or four men who had gathered about me to fire upon them, & shouting at the same time "bring up the whole regiment!" as loudly as I was able, the enemy's party beat a hasty retreat.[13]

As the war was reaching its climax, the general wrote of an encounter with Ulysses S. Grant, general-in-chief and future president, and his wife Julia. The battle-hardened veteran officer from Michigan cited a common experience—all three having lived in Detroit during more bucolic days:

> General Grant came with Mrs. Grant. I arose and bowed to Mrs. Grant. The General announced my name to her, but did not bow or speak to me himself, which I thought very queer—He sat down and seemed fatigued, but this did not seem to me sufficient to account for his silence.

They sat nearly opposite and a few seats above me. In a few minutes Mrs. Grant asked me if I had not been absent on leave, to which I replied with great formality, "Yes, madam, but I returned some days ago." Grant then entered into some conversation, but said not a word nor gave even a look to me, and I now began to feel that his neglect was studied; my heart began to throb and I scarcely tasted any more lunch. In fact, I thought of rising and leaving the table. Fortunately I held on a few moments longer, when he spoke up with his usual cordiality: "Well, Willcox, how did the races come off yesterday?" . . .

Lunch over, I walked over to quarters with the madam . . . and was very much pleased to hear that she remembered so many things and people at Detroit. The General walked on the other side of her, and they both invited me into the hut where they live. So in I walked and had a very pleasant chat with them . . .

I rode home with a light heart after so auspicious an interview and satisfactory results. The six miles to my headquarters seemed scarcely three.[14]

Willcox's war accounts are the most complete of the first Michigan volumes. Ranging from those early days as a boy in frontier Detroit to service as an old man at the veterans' home in the nation's capital, Willcox told one soldier's lifelong tale encompassing most of an entire century. His sense of duty predominated, cultivated from his Michigan roots, even to the point of subverting his own fame. At conflict's end, he had reminded his comrades to "keep high the standard of your honor." His writings proved that he had done so himself. He concluded his remarks at Campus Martius on the Fourth of July 1866 simply: "wishing you every success and prosperity in life, your General bids you a sad but proud Farewell."[15]

It was a goodbye that should not have taken his authorship into obscurity.

Works

. . . .

Shoepac Recollections: A Way-Side Glimpse of American Life (by Walter March, pseudonym) (New York: Bunce & Brothers, 1856).

Faca: An Army Memoir (by Major March, pseudonym) (Boston: James French & Co., 1857).

"West Point: A Tale" (by March, pseudonym), in *Mrs. Stephens' Illustrated New Monthly* 2 (New York; January–June 1857): 30ff.

"Actions on the Weldon Railroad," in *Battles and Leaders of the Civil War*, vol. 4
   (New York: The Century Co., 1884), 568–73.

Forgotten Valor: The Memoirs, Journals & Civil War Letters of Orlando B. Willcox,
   ed. Robert Garth Scott (Kent, OH: Kent State University Press, 1999).

Sites

Campus Martius, Detroit

Southwest corner of Randolph and Larned, Detroit (site of school)

The walkway behind 500 Woodward Avenue, Detroit (Edwin Jerome's school in the
   abandoned university branch building on the west side of Bates between Larned
   and Congress)

South side of Jefferson between Brush and Beaubien, Detroit (site of home)

Capitol Park, Detroit, site of territorial capitol building

Orlando Willcox grave, Arlington National Cemetery, Section 1, Grave 18

Notes

Baker and Thornton: Liberal Artists

1. W. J. Beal, *History of the Michigan Agricultural College: And Biographical Sketches of Trustees and Professors* (East Lansing: Michigan Agricultural College, 1915), 415.
2. Kirkus review of *Under My Elm*, https://www.kirkusreviews.com/book-reviews /david-grayson/under-my-elm/.
3. *(Michigan State College) Record* (East Lansing: July 1946): 4. The cover features a photo and caption "By the Winding Cedar."
4. Philip A. Greasley, ed., *Dictionary of Midwestern Literature*, vol. 1 (Bloomington: Indiana University Press, 2001), 493.
5. This nickname—"Jerry"—came from her husband, though her family knew not why.

Mary Frances Doner: Beyond Bodice Ripping

The works list contains thirty books. The thirty-first might have been a manuscript in her Bentley papers entitled "Bay View Heritage, 1875–1975." The credited author, though, is Keith Fennimore of *The Heritage of Bay View, 1875–1975* (Grand Rapids, MI: Wm. B. Eerdmans Publishing Co., 1975).

1. Obituary, *New York Times*, August 10, 1944.
2. The first entrant: *New York Times* bestseller Nora Roberts.
3. From the dust jacket of *The Darker Star*.
4. *Ludington Daily News*, July 3, 1952, p. 2.
5. Other recipients of dedications included Detroit attorney William Henry Gallagher (*Cloud of Arrows*), who had a role in the *Cleavenger vs. Castle* book, and Blanche Colton Williams, "who believed in me" (*O Distant Star!*).
6. An excellent analysis of her books, especially regarding their Great Lakes connections, is in Greasley, *Dictionary of Midwestern Literature*, 1:145, written by the

esteemed scholar who has invested more than anyone in attending to Doner's work, Professor Emeritus Mary DeJong Obuchowski of Central Michigan University.

7. The title came from a quote from Ralph Waldo Emerson: "Fight best in the shade of the cloud of arrows."

8. Publicity material termed it a glamorous romance set in the rich farmlands of Michigan.

9. A publicity blurb in the May 6, 1940, *Detroit Free Press* says: "Remember the picnics at Belle Isle? The Tashmoo? The Opera House fire? Joe Bedore's? Tashmoo Park? Mary Frances Doner . . . gives a vivid picture of the Detroit of yesterday and today, in this dramatic life story of a courageous woman." The *Tashmoo* was a side-wheel steamer that plied the Detroit and St. Clair Rivers in the early twentieth century. In 2012, a diver found in the St. Clair River a bottle with a message from the ship.

10. This book complained about how Ludington had become the town name as opposed to "Pere Marquette City."

11. The manuscript's original title is *Hometown*, and the subtitle is *A Story of the Dramatic Impact of Urban Renewal on a Great Lakes Town.*

Donald Joseph Goines: A Graphic Life

1. National Public Radio author interview, July 17, 2011. Since his death, sales are reported to have equaled that figure.

2. Quotes in Eddie B. Allen Jr., *Low Road: The Life and Legacy of Donald Goines* (New York: St. Martin's Griffin, 2004), 143–45.

3. Greg Goode, University of Rochester, from the back cover of *Black Girl Lost*.

4. Michael Covino, *Village Voice*, from the back cover of *Eldorado Red*.

5. National Public Radio author interview, July 17, 2011.

6. *Laughter on the Stairs* (Portland, OR: Timber Press, 1998), 134.

James Beardsley Hendryx: Hearty Men and Brave Boys

1. Hendryx's father published the *Sauk Centre Herald*. His mother was a granddaughter of President William Henry Harrison and first cousin of President Benjamin Harrison.

Russell Amos Kirk: Pillar of Tradition

1. That Kirk has had a bibliography published attempting to catalog his work—which required an updated edition after his death—suggests his prodigious impact. Charles Brown, comp., *Russell Kirk: A Bibliography* (Mount Pleasant, MI: Clarke Historical Library, 1981).
2. Aaron McLeod, *Russell Kirk: The Conservative Mind* (Birmingham: Alabama Policy Institute, 2005), 1.

Della Thompson Lutes: Gallant Figure

1. It still operates as the "Detroit Working Writers" group, since 2003 open to male authors. It is Michigan's oldest writers' organization.
2. See *The Writer* (Boston: Writer Publishing Co.) 28 (January 1906): 11.
3. Some sources place Robert's age at seven when the accident occurred. Robert is three when his brother dies, according to *My Boy in Khaki*, 3. Later (6), she writes how she couldn't stand the sight of a gun "in all these fourteen years," which would place the event closer to 1903.
4. Lawrence R. Dawson, "'A Word for What Was Eaten': An Introduction to Della T. Lutes and Her Fiction," *Midwestern Miscellany* 9 (East Lansing, MI: Midwestern Press, 1981), 36.
5. Ibid. Professor Dawson has done the most, it would appear, to keep the Lutes library alive in academic circles.
6. Lawrence R. Dawson, "Della Thompson Lutes: A Preliminary Bibliography," *Bulletin of Bibliography* 39 (December 1982): 184.

Moore and Guest: Hometown Poets

1. Places involving Guest's connections to Detroit, especially downtown, are legion. His first home was at Woodward and Columbia, the street between the Fox and Fillmore Theatres; another in childhood was on Sibley, just north of today's I-75 overpass. He earned pennies watering horses from a fountain at Cass and Clifford. He worked at the Doty Brothers Drug Store at Willis and Woodward Avenues. He began high school at the Biddle House, a hotel converted temporarily to educational purposes when the main high school at Capitol Park burned; today, the Renaissance Center occupies the site. When the new high school opened a year later, Guest attended; today it is known as "Old Main" on the Wayne State University campus.

2. Senate Concurrent Resolution 38, approved March 25, 1952 (*Journal of the Senate of the State of Michigan*, Regular Session of 1952, 1:788), and March 26, 1952 (*Journal of the House of Representatives of the State of Michigan*, Regular Session of 1952, 2:1142).

3. U.S. poet laureate Billy Collins, "Emily Dickinson: An Introduction," in *The Selected Poems of Emily Dickinson* (New York: Modern Library, 2000), xviii.

4. These versions are taken from *The Sentimental Song Book* (New York: Platt & Peck Co., 1912).

5. Ray Cavanaugh, "The Morbid Mrs. Moore," *Michigan History* (March/April 2014): 20–21. Several poems dealt with Civil War subjects.

6. D. B. Wyndham Lewis and Charles Lee, eds., *The Stuffed Owl: An Anthology of Bad Verse* (New York: New York Review Books, 1930), 233.

7. "The Students of the University of Michigan," *The Argonaut* 1 (Ann Arbor: Argonaut Association, 1883), 155.

8. James D. Moore, ed., *The Concise Oxford Companion to American Literature* (Oxford: Oxford University Press, 1986), 271.

9. Http://www.litencyc.com/php/speople.php?rec=true&UID=3179.

10. Walter Blair, ed., *The Sweet Singer of Michigan: Poems by Mrs. Julia A. Moore* (Chicago: Pascal Covici, 1928), xxiv.

11. "When a Little Baby Dies," in *The Path to Home* (Chicago: Reilly and Lee Co., 1919), 155.

12. According to The Henry Ford website, the provenance is this: in 1927, Ford acquired the cart from Colquhoun (nicknamed "Night Owl John"), had it refurbished, and parked it in Greenfield Village to serve as the refreshment stand for visitors, the only place to obtain food. It served as such into the 1930s. Refurbished several times, it is not identical to its nineteenth-century appearance, but still can serve food to patrons, located just behind the Mack Avenue Plant. See http://blog.thehenryford.org/2012/05/hoo-am-i-a-look-at-the-owl-night-lunch-wagon. The connection is in Royce Howes, *Edgar A. Guest: A Biography* (Chicago: Reilly & Lee, 1953), 8–9.

13. Robert Pinsky, "Speaking in Tongues," *Slate*, October 4, 2011.

14. From John S. Terry, ed., *Thomas Wolfe's Letters to His Mother Julia Elizabeth Wolfe* (New York: Charles Scribner's Sons, 1943), 49. The *Argonaut*'s piece including Moore's poem was entitled "The Saccharine Songstress."

15. *A Series of Unfortunate Events #11: The Grim Grotto* (New York: HarperCollins, 2009), 224.

John Tobin Nevill: Unlikely Yooper

1. Lesley Forden, *The Ford Air Tours: 1925–1931* (New Brighton, MN: Aviation Foundation of America, 2003), 186–87.

2. Walter Romig, *Michigan Place Names* (Detroit: Wayne State University Press, 1986), 154. A "tourist" is one who makes a "tour" of places, the latter deriving from the French for "turning, circuit, journey."

3. Obituary of press founder Edward Uhlan, *New York Times*, October 26, 1988.

4. The company had legal difficulties in the 1950s; it was the subject of deceptive marketing prosecutions by the Federal Trade Commission. A federal court found that "Exposition Press, Inc. is a 'subsidy' or 'vanity' publisher. Its business differs from that of most publishing houses in that normally most or all of the expense of publishing its books is paid in advance by their authors. Less than 10% of its authors recoup their investments and derive actual profit from their writing." Perhaps Nevill had the same mindset as the dissenting judge: "Some people think they have written books for which the world is waiting. Publishers who must back judgment with investment take a less sanguine view. Rejection slips accumulate, and frustration mounts. Petitioners are in the business of relieving it." Exposition Press, Inc. v. Federal Trade Commission, 295 F.2d 869 (2d Cir. 1961; Friendly, J., dissenting).

5. See http://www.mackinacbridge.org/prentiss-m.-brown-62. Brown had many "sons," construction workers who for three years labored out of home state pride to fashion the miracle.

6. David B. Steinman, in collaboration with John T. Nevill, *Miracle Bridge at Mackinac* (Grand Rapids, MI: Wm. B. Eerdmans Publishing Co., 1957), 196, 201.

Orlando Bolivar Willcox: Heroic Author

1. Robert B. Ross, *The Early Bench and Bar of Detroit from 1805 to the End of 1850* (Detroit: Joy and Burton, 1907), 224.

2. A distant place beyond the borders of the "known world."

3. The term referred to a foot covering, half shoe and half moccasin, worn by the French settlers.

4. Faca is apparently a nickname for the leading female character.

5. The commendation stated: "Led repeated charges until wounded and taken prisoner."

6. Orlando Bolivar Willcox [Walter March, pseud.], *Shoepac Recollections: A Way-Side Glimpse of American Life* (New York: Bunce & Brothers, 1856), 175.

7. Ibid., 175–76.

8. *Faca* was copyrighted by Willcox and identified the author as having written *Shoepac*. Ironically, it also contained: "Promotion! promotion! give men promotion, or they die!" Orlando Bolivar Willcox [Major March, pseud.], *Faca: An Army Memoir* (Boston: James French & Co., 1857), 96.

9. *Shoepac Recollections*, 32–33.

10. Robert Garth Scott, ed., *Forgotten Valor: The Memoirs, Journals, & Civil War Letters of Orlando B. Willcox* (Kent, OH: Kent State University Press, 1999), xxiv.

11. Sarah Emma Evelyn Edmonds, *Nurse and Spy in the Union Army: Comprising the Adventures and Experiences of a Woman in Hospitals, Camps, and Battlefields* (Hartford, CT: W.S. Williams & Co., 1865 [copyrighted in 1864]).

12. Edward Bacon, *Among the Cotton Thieves* (Detroit: Free Press Steam Book and Job Printing House, 1867).

13. Scott, *Forgotten Valor*, 294–95. Here, and in the next selection, some cosmetic editing has been added.

14. Scott, *Forgotten Valor*, 611–12.

15. Scott, *Forgotten Valor*, 650.